D1516272

This book is radically alive. Visionary, cantankerous, lustful, generously attentive to what Agee called "the common objects of our disregard." Savich writes, "My favorite concept remains the actual, despite everything." Why settle for a life circumscribed by received notions of right and wrong, when you could instead live in the world, "entangle further"? In the tradition of the great poet-teacher treatises before it (think: *Triggering Town, Madness, Rack, and Honey*) *Diving Makes the Water Deep* gifts the reader closer contact with the world by documenting one life's devotion to art.

LISA WELLS

Indicting both the pain and, in equal measure, the gratitude artists feel for the pain, this is a book to remind you that no end has arrived. A book of great sadness, but nothing here is tragic. It's that way where kinship and poetry intersect. The people we meet, Zach's teachers and friends, are each of "intense well-being." And following their model, he too sees the world as warranted, as nothing to correct except in the beauty of our assumptions.

DAVID BARTONE & JEFF DOWNEY

Diving does and does not make the water deep, as Zach says and doesn't say. I am thinking of pain and how much one can let go and give over, as I'm about to go into labor. Which isn't at all like cancer, except my organ has grown an organ, and it will hurt. I'm grateful to this book for being, and asking me to be more, and with.

MELISSA DICKEY

If everything you've ever heard said about poetry was a beautiful forest in which everyone had already dutifully documented every fir and fern, muskrat and butterfly, but no one had ever turned over a single stone on the forest floor and observed what was living on the surface of the soil out of casual notice, then reading this book is like—I know it sounds crazy—getting to breathe the earth beneath that stone.

MARK LEIDNER

This book is incredible. Really incredible. What I mean is, it's not a book at all. It sounds and reads like a gift that sees and pauses and says while I stay listening. It's Zach and thensome.

JORDAN STEMPLEMAN

"All I have left to think is that life is splayed out in all directions and any are certain"—I wrote to Zach once, to feel hope about his health. His book is hope like this, all splayed out and expressive of beautiful and multiple and plying life.

CAREN BEILIN

Out of illness, *Diving Makes the Water Deep* ranges richly across the landscapes of a life's time and spaces, reminding that movement, friendship, and books are reliable miracles; that we're going to lose everything we love; that a tuba is just a piece of metal without your mouth. This is as beautiful and ardent a book as any I can remember, and I want to share it with the people I love.

TYLER MEIER

DIVING MAKES the Water DEEP

RESCUE PRESS
CHICAGO, CLEVELAND, IOWA CITY

Copyright © 2016 Zach Savich
Printed in the United States of America
First Edition
ISBN 978-0-9860869-6-0

Design by Sevy Perez
Illustrations by Christian Patchell
Digital Strip 2.0 BB & Adobe Caslon Pro
rescuepress.co

DIVING MAKES the Water DEEP

ZACH SAVICH

FOR HILARY

By the gate, mosses have grown, the different mosses, too deep to clear them

LI PO

oh my love here even the night turns back

MERWIN

1.

That the poems I wrote before I first had cancer—collected in *Full Catastrophe Living*, *Annulments*, *The Firestorm*, and *Century Swept Brutal*—would not sound right at my memorial.

2.

That the poems I wrote after I first had cancer—in *The Orchard Green and Every Color*—would not sound right anywhere else.

3.

That I have not talked with my students about the various ways of reading poems at memorials who will?

4.

That graceful is any hand to the extent that the sun.

5.

Self-elegy is a critical term, I just learned, don't have time to learn about it.

6.

That when I first had cancer, at thirty, three months after my father died at sixty from the same cancer, I thought of these lines from Larry Levis:

The last thing my father did for me
Was map a way: he died, & so
Made death possible. If he could do it, I
Will also, someday, be so honored

7.

I started saying it without the final phrase, preferring to end on "someday." In the rooms of explicit examination, this week, I've felt the passage is beautiful but hardly true. The last thing my father did for me was die and so took care of that. I can focus elsewhere. Much as he knew the name of any tree, so I could simply look. (Paper covering the elevated examination bed, too thin to write on: a part of my body, you could take it between your fingers, go ahead.)

8.

I've felt differently: my father's father died in his forties, from the same cancer, and my father proved he could live. If my father's answer to his father's death was to live, I used to think, my answer could be to accept dying.

9.

Marcus Aurelius: a life, of any length, is one-hundred percent of a life.

10.

That I first read Marcus Aurelius as an undergraduate teaching assistant in Hal Opperman's Ideas in Art course, University of Washington, 2003. I was, somehow, twenty. A course pairing books—Freud, Whitman, Alberti—with slides of paintings, dance stills, stone. Hal presented one day a week. I led discussion the next. In the Aurelius session, I rejected the philosopher-emperor's detachment. He says, for instance, that if you find yourself enchanted by a melody, save yourself like this: consider each note of the melody in turn, and ask if it alone enchants you, and thus be spared from harm. But if I am enchanted by the melody, when I consider each note in turn, the answer must be yes already.

11.

It was fall, I lived with Molly on Eastlake, water past condos not yet built. I can feel the exact motion of rearing my bicycle into the elevator, fog, cars on an overpass at some hours blocking sun, mail through the door's slot. I left my research job each afternoon at the Center for Educational Leadership and Policy Studies—I worked for Ken Sirotnik, who died of cancer the next year, contributing to his book about the drawbacks of standardized testing, quaint warning cry now—leaving early to sit on a low wall until she appeared through the leaves. The anticipation and seeing: acute. Path before the bride appears. Walk now together over the drawbridge home. With luck it is open and we have to wait and see boats.

12.

That Ken did not correct my research's lyrical prose (I was taking a Joyce seminar with Nikolai Popov, reading Hopkins's journals, believed it was treasonous, given the possibilities of language, to settle for less than the most vivacious possibilities of language). I remember, teaching now, all the teachers who did not correct me. Let the students surge incorrectly let them prove us wrong or at least different and continue.

13.

That I most recently read Marcus Aurelius in 2006, Paris. Waiting for my friend to finish class and let me back into her apartment. Drinking espresso so slowly I didn't need to swallow, it became my mouth. I wrote one line about every painting I saw and then did the same in the street: what sight isn't a painting.

14.

Weeks later, Rome: I lectured on Aurelius. He says beauty results from the "incidentals of nature's processes." Cracks baking leaves in a

loaf, figs at the final instance of ripening, saliva hot on a lion's jaws.
I can't picture those jaws—nonchalant instance—without seeing
a person there. Hero or slave or clown—a figure for the poet, I
said. We the cracks baking leaves in a loaf. You'd lose your head for
it. It connects, I said, to Pound's saying such-and-such is "of the
process," this other such-and-such is "of the process." To find what
is of the process, that is poetics enough. (Poetry is data processing,
but you don't know what the data is or what data is or how to process.) (The difference between poetry and prose is prose.)

15.

That when I first had cancer, spring 2013, two years ago, I canceled
teaching in Rome but exchanged letters with a student who went.
He wrote, "I tried to buy two sprigs of grapes in the market but
they gave me two kilos." Carried them to class in his shirt. Ordinary miracle. And how endearing: his asking for sprigs. What word
or gesture did he use?

16.

He was reading Keats's letters, noted how frequently Keats begins
by apologizing for the delay in correspondence. He derived a
theory about writing and language and eros from it. I did not
correct him, though of course this is how everyone's letters begin. I
preferred his theory and his having it. I'm sorry it has been so long
since I've written.

17.

Those Levis lines, though, on mapping a way. During my illness, I was grateful for certain sufferings: they must have been my father's sufferings. A way to be closest to his last months, transliteral resurrection. But I feel he is no longer my guide, I am past his maps now, I imagine him shrugging if I ask for advice, we are friends in the unknown and unsayable, in that moment when Virgil becomes just another poet strolling with Dante and Statius and the pagan lady: Paradise is a didactic shambles compared to that amble in Purgatory with those friends, that conversation.

18.

That cadence—borrowed from Roethke, about a father's death: "What need for heaven, with that man, and those roses?"

19.

I will not look up the lineation, I know the words. And I realize I'm echoing Roethke doubly, perhaps doubly obliquely, since he also says, "I take this cadence from a man named Yeats."

20.

That the ideas I had during health seem merely expressions of health. And my ideas now?

21.

That for many years I railed against preemptive elegy, those violins, art of no other aesthetic but the dying ache, any example instantly a memento mori. The sadness of emblematic bananas. Anyone who has loved or read even shallowly already knows we are dying this is brief there is more to see the harder part the better part is living is saying what's next next.

22.

"*Here* is the time for the sayable," says Rilke in the translation I prefer. Not "*now* is the time."

23.

Now must be the place.

24.

Cancer: similar memento. Say it and conditions that should be obvious, ever-present, to anyone who has loved or read—that we are fragile, impermanent, not in control, afflicted with unreasonable joy in the midst—become a story you can tell, external. But I still prefer experiences that are not easily worded. The experience of cancer is not "cancer." The unapparent is still larger. To say "oh, I know what that is like, I know what you mean"—a way to not see.

25.

Facts never overlap, in other words. Each tree is a tautology, and once again if you circle it another way.

26.

That I never recovered from my first cancer. If I live, I will never recover even more. How often can you drink from these waters with only your hand.

27.

That since moving to Philadelphia—after the initial bout—I have met many people I adore, but I fear—have I acted strangely, or not shown it enough, not shown up enough, because of being steadily sick, unable? Someone advertises a marathon reading, a party that starts at nine, I can't imagine.

28.

That despite believing differently, I still sometimes associate illness with morality. Because who would believe anything I say, seeing where it has led? My diagnosis refutes me. And I sometimes wish others would be refuted, suffer more. Not just people I disdain—like the "TED talk luminary" I heard on NPR this morning, saying most diseases are caused by kids being raised like sissies, without hearty frontier bootstrap values, though I turned off the radio before he answered the host's next idiotic question ("from the perspective of evolutionary biology, how do you explain Islamic terrorism?")—but also the targets of minor gripes. An author on Facebook says her novel's ranking has fallen on Goodreads, due to it being ranked by people who read it. Could her friends please help pump the ranking back up? As though literature is nothing but the summoning of such networks.

29.

That I still hold on to petty hurts, despite illness. There was the colleague at my old job who, after my father died, leaving behind my mother, his wife of forty years, to care for my disabled sister, suggested that it would be a good opportunity for my mom to liberate herself from the rule of a man.

30.

This colleague was very lonely. When she went through a breakup, I gave her Maggie Nelson's *Bluets*. She read it and said how could a book purportedly about color not discuss issues in Asian-American diaspora (this colleague's field)? I saw the point, and have since raised a related one when teaching the book; and the moon has the nerve to not be the sun. (What to make of criticism that says the problem with one thing is that it is not everything, or even a potential set of possible other things? The problem with one life.)

31.

Not letting go, not making peace, not pretending a book covers everything or expecting one life to: a form of staying alive.

32.

"It's not the dying but the disentangling," my father kept saying. Meaning: we should wish for further entangling, entangle, entangle and surge. The melody is already enchanting and already not endless enough already why not sing several.

33.

He did not seem afraid to die. He was afraid to die before finishing my wife's novel.

34.

He asked me to buy the best whiskey. Wanted a smell. Then asked for a sip, vomited. I don't think vomiting disproved the pleasure of the sip.

35.

I've mentioned drinking and the new cancer is in my liver, so someone will think you get cancer in the liver at thirty-two because of drinking. You get it because of Lynch syndrome, a genetic mutation. (It's likely this cancer has been with me since the first cancer, sooner, what doesn't date back further than even giant ferns or mule elk in the spruce.) My condition's most poetic name? Microsatellite instability.

36.

That he made a chart of the wines in the basement: here is when to drink each. An amateur interest. He acknowledged that many might not age well, but they'd be interesting to try.

37.

That there are thousands of poems I would like to show my students.

38.

That I don't trust how most people teach poetry and hate the thought of them with my students, even as I love them for taking over my classes.

39.

That I want to read the poems students will be writing in twenty years—my current students, future students—more than what currently publishing poets will be writing. Many poets around eighty or so have been dying lately; people mourn this, I do too, though eighty seems lucky. How many currently publishing poets will keep writing, caring, deepening, for even a decade, let alone until they are eighty, let alone luckily. Is that a goal. What would I write today if so.

40.

That I railed against literature about dead fathers. Against the teacher who told a student that her story should be about fathers and sons and dying, like his stories were. Against the students in a graduate workshop who wrote only about fathers and dying. (Their fathers were alive, it was an aesthetic, or, at least, a rehearsal—but why rehearse what will happen anyway? Why not just call their dads and talk and write about that? They also liked to include lists of hardscrabble ditch detritus, sensitive tough catalogues of stock condom wrappers beer bottles cigarette butts epiphany. But what about the people.)

41.

Who else did I rail against, for example at the Spoke after workshop with free meatballs in the slow cooker by the gumball machine in Massachusetts? How about the graduate student who said he couldn't "relate" to a poem about death because he had never known anyone who died.

42.

He had never known Emily Dickinson?

43.

This student titled a poem "Spring," he said, because everyone around him seemed excited about the season. Immune to spring and death: this is not a poet I care about. (He was the young dude I've met in several MFA programs interested in "comedy" as a way to avoid being interested in reading or things, and so he could tell others to lighten up.) (Also of course if the writing is good and you greet it you can relate to anything tales of the moon cookbooks of food you never imagined.)

44.

That I was generally against memoirs about dying parents, especially the inevitable moment when the narrator-child wipes the parent's ass, sees genitals. Seeing my father's scrotum swollen around his penis, gray sores of the ass, loose light brown liquid shit which soon became how I shit—that was among the easiest parts of his dying. You shift the balls, blot the ass. If that was all it took, dying would be as simple as changing a tire.

45.

Against the glee you feel the writer feeling at such an obvious "scene," one they can recognize instantly as meaningful, if you (wrongly) take meaningful to mean you can explain what the mean-ing is (I cannot explain the meaning of the most meaningful things, we live them, their meaning exceeds my explanation what does it mean to love what do sunsets and sufferings mean). Meanwhile ignoring (diminishing) the less apparent all around.

46.

That I feel pleasure, respect, in witnessing the intelligence and skill and compassion of my doctors, even though it is my illness that has revealed it.

47.

That it is a standard phrase, to say one will do anything to help. But I believe it, believe my friends would, they would, they will, they have lived strangely and creatively to generously now offer this. If you wish to criticize the arts or creative writing programs, please know that some real outcomes of the arts and creative writing programs are these people who in my illness have begun to appear, to call, to read to me when I can't, to bring food. But there is actually little to ask. Send me news from your life.

48.

Around the time my father last lost consciousness, he visited me in a dream. Intense well-being, embrace. Then I was suddenly seeing myself: meaning I was seeing with his eyes, perhaps would from now on. I woke weeping, not because I believed his dying soul visited me in a dream, but because I believed if it had been possible to, after petitioning the appropriate heavenly offices, trading against whatever resources the dead can vow, he would have. That's love's tense: not *is* but *would*.

49.

"We fight for what we love, not are," says O'Hara.

50.

"If it would only hail in jewelry stores," says Breton. Surrealism, I said in a lecture another summer in Rome, is not about the hail in jewelry stores, that glitzy image. It's about the desire that causes a metamorphosis, requires it, given the world, which can't accommodate one's desire. What matters is the "if it would only." That is the catalyst. Not is, would.

51.

"I would lie to you / If I could," says James Wright, in "To the Muse," a poem I read my father in his hospice bed.

52.

Wright, who said craft is the passionate contention with love and death.

53.

Who I read at nineteen in a rough time. And decided very simply.
Poetry had saved my life. So I would give my life to poetry. The easiest thing. And so everything happened.

54.

Of course a person who would make that resolution is enchanted
already, not least by the syntax ("x has saved my life, and so I will give
my life to x"). Such a person might give his life for the chance to say
such a phrase.

55.

There are many books I would like to read. I see the gaps in my
canon, my teachers, my past, feel them too well, as shame, as wishing
I had more time. But these are the lines I know, have been made by,
years I rarely bought books (moving too often, little money), so you
made everything you read a part of you. And now are marked, without time. This is what you can do while you can, so you do. The edge
appears and we speak. I believe the abyss is lush with lichens.

56.

The archaic word for "refrain," I say any chance I get, is "burden." The
part of the song we carry, it carries.

57.

Some days, teaching, it doesn't even take a wicked etymology to
make language feel magical—to say "refrain" means "burden," or
that a "companion" is one you share bread with, each word a poem.
Defining "etymology" can be magical enough.

58.

It's a compass with three norths, Rick said, in the first poetry class I
took. Language is a sensory organ. Passing ideas, he didn't explain,
but they stuck. I have since lived to see.

59.

But he didn't answer the question I wrote on the first day of class. He
answered other students'—how do you know when a poem is done,
how do you come up with titles. But not mine: what should poetry
be accountable to? We have been talking about it one way or another
ever since. ("Next life," he says in one poem, "do it in prose." This life
has been poems. In which the answer, the accounting, turns line by
line, more actual than actuarial.)

60.

Rome, 2007, again teaching, in the program I attended as an
undergraduate, Rick's program. City as classroom, poetry as

ambulation, synthesis, all subjects. He suggested (in response to some theories of difficulty I was enamored with) but maybe poetry should be accountable to the recently dead, accessible to them, not just to a specialist reader. (This is how we talked, people talk like this, we were walking to a student poetry reading at dusk on the Capitoline, artichokes afterward at a restaurant famous for them and a nearby juggler.) I have heard others say this: suffering and loss have caused them to prefer simpler art. But suffering has made me want only more and more from art. When I imagine myself or my dead resurrected for the duration of a poem, consciousness and world composed again by nothing but the text, their standards are very high. Experiment, comedy, intelligence, wildness, distinct disorientation—they want it all at the hardiest. To access something further through.

61.

The intimate, the private, the unapparent. The writerly. Not celebrity, not product, not performance that supersedes (without reaching the extent of theater), not branding, not a guru, not expression measured more by familiarity than rightness or implosion or beauty. In so many books I see only the writer's ambition to be seen as a certain kind of writer, receive certain invitations—I yawn. Aspects lyricism is better suited to resist. (Some desire better clichés; and that's rhetoric? And what is it to desire, more even than honesty, maybe, something other than cliché?)

62.

That despite having published five books, I have published only first
books. I am beginning. Or now does every book become a last book.

63.

Divergence becomes a type of coherence, Dean Young told me in
graduate school. Also: that I didn't need to decide about poetics
except poem by poem, line by line. But I sometimes worry my work
is diluted by its variety, it's frivolous. Some reviewers agree: I like
this kind of poem in his book, they say, but not this other kind, why
can't it all be the same? Though who would feel such a thing among
the grapes of an outdoor market or the world.

64.

The love of simplicity is the love of death, Rick said, or I did, or
a student did. In favor of the baroque, the implicated. Let us be
implicated, implicated, entangled more.

65.

I'm not the first to say it: how often I prefer the banter at a poetry
reading, and then the poet reads poems that excise, purify, de-
hydrate, polish off all personality and stammering and uncertain

ecstasy or undisclosable poise. I enjoy the after-party, and emailing later, nevertheless.

66.

I wouldn't trust anyone who's not afraid of public speaking, I tell students who are nervous about reading aloud. It has been said often but needs to keep being said: the most poetic performance is the language itself, if you believe in language, a performance that exists in its way in any accent, any setting, changes each time, yes, but is of the words in the mouth, not just the mouth. Though plenty still act as though screaming "I love you" in stage makeup is more meaningful than whispering it close, that a marriage would mean more if it were accessible to the widest public conventions, if its language were closer to advertising, its flavor to commercial jerky, here I am speaking from the gut, as though sincerity can't also be stupid and short-sighted and cruel. Or I could tell you something I have never heard or said and don't quite understand. That is how much I love you. Enough to say "I love you" in another phrase.

67.

But I've become sympathetic to the love of simplicity in new ways. In this suffering, I prefer action movies in which the hero not only inevitably triumphs but is hardly ever hit. The other night some friends debated in which decade Steven Seagal was last hit.

68.

I knew someone with similar taste: Jeff's housemate, Massachusetts. He spent most evenings riding a stationary bike while playing video game football, set the game so his team could win by a predictable hundred. He flinched when we watched movies in which the hero was ever in danger. Of course I judged him. An innocent, I declaimed: isn't it better to prefer complexity, difficulty, the thick of life, even its losses? As though one has a choice, as though preference matters, as though his preference didn't come from pains I couldn't see.

69.

I want this, you gotta want this enough, says the standard reality TV line. The standard cultural line. As though desire is deserving, as though it's your fault when you don't get everything. The unemployed don't want employment enough, those without drinking water don't want it enough. I didn't want to not have a recurrence of cancer enough. If my poems had been better, if my thinking had been sharper...

70.

Or (you still hear this) God doesn't give you more than you can bear, and God doesn't give the recent victims of massacre more than they can bear, and God definitely doesn't give malnourished children more than they…

71.

How have I been writing all this time without hearing the rain on my window. Listening now I can smell it, and the sidewalk, trees. If you want to stay here, according to myth, you should eat everything you are offered, in case this is already the underworld.

72.

That before I first had cancer, I was preoccupied with the afterlife, because I suddenly had a job with stability, more money than I had ever made, but which felt lifeless.

73.

I had always (naively) (Puritanically) (self-hurtingly) thought I could live anywhere, find or make the astonishment and agitation I needed, especially if I was teaching, able to teach as I liked. Had long vowed to never be like the professors who complain. Like when I was adjuncting and working in a warehouse, and I ran into a colleague in the copy room, and he complained about needing to teach a class or two each semester to interested students. Professors who complain about sometimes needing to go to a meeting, or to meet with students. Of course thinking of my father never working fewer than however many, many hours a week except during his dying, I resolved, I resolved. (One friend, who teaches at a large university that enjoys regarding itself as elite, hearing me talk about my struggling composition students, their alienation from and skepticism about the university, the fallout of their early educations and having come of age in our economy and wars, told me he'd always found teaching Jane Austen helped vitalize a difficult first-year writing course. I believe he viewed most of what higher education is as below his due.)

74.

But in that hard job I learned. For several weeks, my closest friend was a sausage sandwich lasting impossibly long on a bench. I checked on it most days. If it could last in that town, I, too, could be so honored.

75.

My other friend at the time. A woman I'd see on the trail, under the overpass. Well-dressed, bicycle leaning against a pylon. Spending her days, smoking. I'd nod walking past. Or say hello in a way that granted privacy, which is to say, that established intimacy. Could a poem grant readers such privacy? Trying to be a poet who wrote about silos.

76.

Taught at a local poetry festival, hoping to meet, say, a high-school
teacher in her mid-thirties, have an affair. I drove home a woman in
her eighties. Widow of a famous painter. She showed me hundreds
of pages she'd written, explaining the universe: I wished I could
believe in her system. I'm sorry I did not go back to see her.

77.

Every story can be summarized "I told a story about it."

78.

But now that Levis poem seems unforgivable:

This isn't the whole story.
The fact is, I was still in love.
My father died, & I was still in love. I know
It's in bad taste to say it quite this way.

Because of course a father dies and we are still in love. I am thinking
about tacos at the funeral, still in love, I am eating tacos mere hours
later, still in love, I am with my beautiful friend with taco breath, in love
and still in love, I am dying with taco sauce on my fingers, in love. These
are only contradictions if you expect a love of simplicity that is a love

of death, otherwise there is only entangling, entangling, thank you, yes.

79.

The other singular dream I had, the night before my father last lost consciousness: Jake Adam York, the poet, dead several months before, at forty, was waiting for him at a campfire. I woke crying, not because I thought Jake's spirit was waiting to meet my father in the afterlife but because of how much they would have enjoyed meeting in this life.

80.

The sharpest grief: how much my father would have enjoyed talking with any of my friends. Don't ask him about death or the afterlife, tell him about your day.

81.

The only way I can understand what thinking is: talking in your head to people who are not here. I can't grasp the concept separate from imagining you listening, so then I'm listening.

82.

That in some ways my mother's car not starting a few weeks after he died was harder to bear than his death.

83.

Another University of Washington professor who died of cancer: Jim Clowes, who counseled me when my highest ambition, in more than all seriousness, was to sit under trees reading. I thought I'd have more liberty to do so outside of school. I am grateful to those who didn't correct me and to Jim for telling me to stick around, but to stick around as though I had already left.

84.

Before he died, he gave a final lecture. He warned against thinking you know. In favor of contradiction, attention, unknowing.

85.

When my father was first finally dying, he said basically the same. Ideas are scars from past experiences. Ideas are already past. This is something else.

86.

That I do not wish to give a final lecture, commencement address, statement that will be touching if projected at a memorial. I'd rather say it wrong then say more another time. The last words being all of them, to always make an awkward bow.

87.

That I take (smug, maudlin) pleasure in being mannerly toward doctors and nurses. They compliment how articulate I am. I enjoy receiving and reporting this praise.

88.

That, in the midst of this, someone online is mad because poets read their work in an affected style. As though poetry isn't at its heart style, affectation. As though any reading style isn't affected (some affects are more fashionable this afternoon). As though I'd complain, were she resurrected for an off-site event at AWP, about Emily Dickinson's reading style, however she sounded. It's the perfect complaint for our era, since it's all about personality, social projection, social herding of a "community," avoidance of actual talk about writing, avoidance of issues in the world (this writer jailed…), avoidance of contention with love and death (craft). I wish for the poets that I love that they have more time to write, to write better, to love writing—not that they become more consumable entertainment. (Last night we read Notley in the kitchen, we needed it: there is the performance. For those poems, in that hour, no voice would have been wrong.)

89.

For years I'd earnestly ask friends, after a disappointing reading, when they were excited by the reading, what they loved about it. Out of my desire to desire more. I have stopped asking this question, just as I have stopped thinking that my "community" is everyone who happens to share my interest in poetry, rather than my neighbors, coworkers, friends. Why can't poets just say "scene" like punk rockers used to? What's a we.

90.

Just as I have stopped earnestly asking—what's wrong with valuing (romanticism/forms fashionable in another year/seemingly out-of-date or nascent theories/whatever), despite aspects of those elements, their usage, having been critiqued or used wrongly? But we can prefer correctives to what's correct. E.g., it is a good corrective to say we shouldn't overvalue the effusions of an expressive self. But there is still an expressive self, and effusiveness, and if there isn't, why am I shouting? Having often been wrong, changed my mind, I don't expect these ideas—anyone's—to hold, let us have time to move on, apologize.

91.

Vestigial coolness, anxiety, more concern with proving a thesis (a persona) than with conversation. The desire to be critically unassailable. (Let me be a sail.)

92.

Pain on inhalation. Experiment with trying to breathe only outward? Worsening for weeks. You realize inhalation is inseparable from exhalation, not a cycle, a single ceaseless motion: pain steadily. Low fever for a month. Exhaustion, disclarity, night sweats, hobbled, hunched. I heard a change in my doctor's voice, in which I heard Keats's phrase, when he coughed the blood he'd seen his brother cough—"I know that blood." Arterial. The exact nature of things is unknown yet troublingly urgent.

93.

That several professors (older, dudely, employed at more boringly revered institutions than I've ever napped in), when I said I spent much of my first year in my new job unwell, on the floor of my office, replied that ha ha they spent a good part of their first years teaching like that too ha ha. Immediate diminishment, shift back to their own suffering, important busyness. But you didn't have cancer, I wanted to say. Shift back to my suffering.

94.

That when it was especially bad, I'd find, in the middle of a class, that I couldn't remember more than what had just happened. I trusted that if I focused enough, responded intently to the immediate, didn't worry about anticipating, gave up any canned banter, there would be continuity in the discussion. I think it made better discussions.

95.

Grateful for the times hungover, fucked up, exhausted from staying up fucking, and needing to pass in the world. It taught me I could survive, and so I might today. Pleasure prepares us.

96.

That I believe I am talking and thinking about poems with more insight/significance than ever before. Only just now beginning to see. The net of text holds itself out.

97.

That the tests will reveal information but will not change the pain.

98.

That my favorite concept remains the actual, despite everything. I believe that insisting on that, as on the *experiential* reality of language, is ethical and consequential and a way of making a world (a corrective?).

99.

You enter another country and don't know the language and are exhausted. But you'd be wrong to blame the country or the language or to long for familiar sentences, phrases your dead father made. Instead: sleep, find coffee, a mouth you don't mind watching. Follow it through bicycles and trees. Learn a joke, a curse, song, sounds that are enough to see. I do not want a theory about life but more life. I do not want to "understand" if that means checking this country off my list, got it, no need to see what's happening by the docks this week, what new words, I know what I think. Wanting cosmography, not cosmology. Periplum is poetics enough. The figure is the same for poetry as it is for love, says Frost, is poetics enough (given the addition of Creeley: what is love today?).

100.

That the rain has stopped so the sky seems both darker and more inviting, I would go out in it.

1.

"Even the business of dying must be set aside occasionally," says D.A. Powell.

2.

"The industry of flowers / Is dying young," says James Galvin. And: "The body floats / Face down in the soul." (I'm going by memory, all errors are mine.)

3.

That Galvin, as my teacher, told me what poetry should be accountable to. It had to do with a field.

4.

And underlined "merciless" in my final critical paper, without explanation. I didn't take it as commentary but meditation. His comments at the end went, roughly, "This is a pretty good paper. However, I don't think you've grappled fully with Milton and Blake." The paper was not about Milton or Blake, and how many people have grappled fully with them? A good comment.

5.

That Powell talked to me in the corner of a party, instead of to the poets I thought were famous poets. I was graduating from the MFA at Iowa. I had made no plans, done nothing but read and write and fall in love for two years. He said now wait five years, maybe more. Didn't say for what. Good advice.

6.

Oh, but while I was in a painkiller nap just now, I remembered how annoyed I've been lately by poets who giddily claim contemporary life (especially the internet) is boring and write boring poetry about their boring days and search histories and how diminished and mundane current life is to prove it, every dull phrase an earnest authenticity of dull evidential dullness. I feel sorry for them, they don't have friends and search histories as interesting as mine, only acolytes who interview them and repeat, feel good about being on the inside, having a stance, being of (only) a moment. What international news and medical ailment blogs and ASMR videos and enthusiasms are they ignoring? Why do they prefer this vision, given the possibility for language and thought to be more than something they have figured out by learning not to see, and especially if they aren't sick or jailed or? Who am I talking about, anyway? They are surely the past by now.

7.

When I first had cancer, I was too sick to read Roberto Bolaño's
"Literature + Illness = Illness," but I was grateful for the title. Thank
you, Roberto Bolaño, for understanding that the sick need your
writing, too, even if they can't read past the title.

8.

The title helped me ignore the lamer memoirs of suffering that
people send when you have cancer. One suggested I get a pet turtle.
Another endorsed a revolutionary juicer.

9.

I dismissed those memoirs by composing a poem called "The
Memoirs of the Sick," after Mary Ruefle's "The Philosophy of the
Astonished." Her poem starts: "I don't know how the astonished can
have / a philosophy since they can't speak." I don't know how the sick
can write memoirs…

10.

On my birthday, the year before my father died, I read poems at
a college near my parents' house. I was revved, grateful to stretch

rhetorically while mired in my shitty job, where many propositions in class or committee had to be hoisted on a stool with two legs of bullshit. I spoke incredibly quickly. A couple of students came up afterward and asked me for the poems I'd read, seemed like they'd be glad to spend the evening with me stupid on a nearby bluff, but the organizers seemed uncertain. I had failed at networking, at being smooth. Or were they just tired, in their lives, the night another required event? I worried afterward that I had spoken too incredibly quickly. My father said, "It wasn't too fast for me."

11.

Smooth, networking. Do you remember when a major-ish magazine called New York City "'literature's largest stage'?" Literature's largest stage is the pupal.

12.

Do you remember a website that was not a parody I'm pretty sure featuring throbbing photos of Brooklyn poets that claimed Brooklyn was the birthplace of poetry?

13.

In Brooklyn, after giving a reading, I introduced myself to some people at the after-party. Wishing to be friendly, not knowing anyone, from out of town. Tried it twice and received handshakes without people saying their names. Like I was supposed to already know? Like it (I) didn't matter? (I could see that, sure, sure…) They were talking about a poet who people like to use the nickname of, suggesting intimacy/power, as though the poet was a more important celebrity than any of us, as though talking about them was the best we could hope for, unless someone more famous walked into the room. Or maybe they knew the poet, which was intimacy/power and I wasn't part of it? I don't know. I could've been the problem, and left. Is this contemporary prosody.

14.

That you get used to canceling plans, then to not making them, not having the energy to even imagine. You calculate when in the day to buy coffee, to get through: amazed at those reading in a café. As though coffee is a way to pass time, not a necessary boost. Then even the ability to be there, wondering—it's also gone.

15.

You need to decide if you'll take the early train and have time to sleep on the floor of your office or take the later train and have time to stay in bed longer. How to rest enough.

16.

An invitation to dinner and drinks. Means three hours, four? And being thirty minutes from home. Worth the exhaustion? What does it do to you, to always be calculating the worth?

17.

Or you feel well, and remain stupid enough—even if it's only an hour!—to think this means you will never suffer again, maybe no one will. Do you expend energy while you can (could lead to a worse crash) or try to save it (will also lead to a crash)?

18.

In college, I'd read *Illness as Metaphor* and *The Body in Pain* and *Darkness Visible* and *Autobiography of a Face*, and I knew about Kant's gout (he said that concentrating on thought was the only palliative) and Bernini placing his hand in a flame, watching his face in a mirror to sculpt embodied agony. So I knew things could be *said* about suffering, and that to read such books could offer—not relief, but alleviation? Less salvage or salvation than salve? But I cannot stomach the popular accounts of affliction.

19.

But by this point I am missing most of my (bada-bing) stomach!

20.

Problems with memoirs of the sick. Treating narrative as a structure, rather than a struggle. Showing affliction then insight, as though insight (presented as inseparable from tired narrative patterns) can save us. Fucking redemption. Isn't every work of art about suffering? So illness memoirs are redundant.

21.

What I wanted from memoirs of the sick. Affliction but/yet insight. You can have any insight you want, but you are still in a body, in time, in Netflix and opiates and the horrifying, unmoderated online forum of the heart. But who wouldn't trade any of illness's insights for a day of health? You should be sensitive to the ways in which telling a story, believing it, seeing yourself as a main character, especially one who can face affliction with joy or resolve—all that depends on abilities that are hard to maintain when your body is altering, pain deep. I mean, didn't I often wish for the ability to believe in a story or an idea, to believe it could stand to the bandages and scans, more than I wished for a specific story or idea? The real subject should be dealing with pain and time.

22.

So I did what I do and remembered poems.

23.

My method was to establish myself in the backyard and remember poems until I got a little ecstatic, then I'd collapse. The rest of the day, the ceiling fan kept me alive.

24.

One poem I remembered was "Cries" by Henri Michaux (trans. Ellman). It starts: "The pain of an abcessed finger is excruciating." But Michaux— it would be inane to call him "the speaker"—can't cry out, because he's in a hotel, people are sleeping. So, he pulls "great drums, brasses, and an instrument which had more resonance than an organ" from his skull, making a "deafening orchestra of them." In this pandemonium, he is able "to scream for hours on end," and thus, in his mind, gains some relief.

25.

The poem says that art can mask suffering? Or that it can convey it, secretly, in a way that exceeds and contains the original volume of one's cries, while being socially OK, a formal feeling that can get integrated back into any day's to-do? Today I think it's saying that we are often abruptly altogether elsewhere, via the ordinary instantaneousness of the imagination, not in a metaphor but in a poem. The orchestral trepanation seems almost painless, though not without suffering.

26.

Of course, one could also say: it's almost painless, because impossible. This is not a story of relief from suffering. It is a story of the dream of relief from suffering. The impossibility of which is another form of suffering, but not without relief. A song of innocence.

27.

That I first read "Cries" in a park in Paris, waiting for my friend. Is this the kind of thing that still happens in the world? Somebody is carrying a cantaloupe he will eat with a knife swiped from a noodle joint, reading Henri Michaux? You know I bought many noodles, many winding bowls of steam, before stealing that knife. Of course it barely cut the rind.

28.

Healthy enough, those days, to wish for days in which I could do nothing but read. I have since had such days.

29.

That I read the poem to Steve in Rome. This is all still 2006. He delighted at the word "abcessed." He was my roommate and hero. We had an apartment near the train station, excellent balcony, vines. Sometimes he'd disappear, show up in the evening with two beautiful fish.

30.

Illness disrupts the coherent autobiographical self (always a fiction, always more real than it seems, as fiction also is), the persona that workaday "creative nonfiction" depends on. You become a disease and its doctors. Do they care how many books I've written, the invitations I had to teach a class here, give a reading there, scheduled for this very canceled instant? Sometimes one tells me he's fond of Robert Frost as I go under.

31.

Consider suffering's simultaneous self-absorption and incitement to empathy. The former refigures the self by reducing you to symptoms, conditions, enduring. The latter refigures the self by expanding it.

32.

The pain I feel is worse to me than any other, because it is mine. And yet, during any moment of suffering, I also know that your (somebody's) suffering is worse. Each pain reveals another depth of pain I can't imagine, each pain reveals only itself.

33.

In an appropriate memoir of illness, the self would become multiple, roving, restless, empathetic, and also anchored to its abysmal sensations, which have no qualities of character, history, mind, yet are highly personal, strangely receptive, in annihilating and expanding senses.

34.

It's like my idea of the locative obliterative. For example, walking home late one night, someone tried to hustle Steve's wallet in a drunken dance, grabbing his belt, pulling him off balance while another thief came from behind. Steve pushed them away. It had nothing to do with him—he could've been anyone—but there he was, hand on his belt. It would be wrong to take it personally. Even if the event was personal, it was in a larger structural/historical/cultural way than a plain "personal narrative" could relate.

35.

Much art operates by a locative obliterative principle. A trompe l'oeil, for example, with illusions that depend on (and deepen with) your angle, visual experience, perception. But also have nothing to do with you. You're nothing next to them, or you are something else.

36.

I should mention that for many years I felt calmest in bustling Rome, because of this. (I have been told every creature has its camouflage moment.)

37.

Pleasure prepares us: memoirs of the sick should acknowledge this.

Learning to piss again, after surgery, I remembered a night Dan drove me to a field of lightning. High spirits: I felt anything could happen, I could vomit, shit, sing, bleed, fall among the alfalfa and fireflies. He wouldn't mind. He counted between flash and thunder.

38.

I braced myself in the hospital—bleeding, falling—and pictured that field, a flash. Hear him count.

39.

Or with Steve on a slow sweaty train. Hours in, for the absurdity of further heat (one answer to being trapped in heat), we moved to an improbable plexiglass compartment. Sealed ourselves in. Smoked the cigarettes old men smoke, drank hot white wine, traded clothes with some Germans. An Italian puppeteer in a trench coat joined. He and I were in a heated agreement about the necessity of chaos in art, especially in landscape, especially in regions of historic dairy production. Until I realized he wasn't saying "chaos" but "cows." Ten years ago.

40.

Or other preparations that have existed in the world. 2002. With a woman from Israel, on a beach. She placed stones on my body, as they had to her in the desert. It was supposed to sink you into earth,

teach you, and then the stones would be removed, and you'd feel
yourself rise. Levitate a little.

41.

At the time I felt only her hands. Through the stones. Her hands
through the stones occasionally lingering where my body or the
stones wished most.

42.

Years later, in the hospital, I finally felt the rocks, and the sinking,
then the greater rising. Thank you, person I didn't know how to love
at the time because I had to learn that kind of loving by failing at
loving you at the time.

43.

Another thing I wanted from memoirs of the sick: to see the severe
wild bliss I felt, in recovery, that was distinct from the gratitude of
survival, from animal fondness, from sensation and appetites returning. I tried to describe it to a friend. "Right," she said, "like in Blake."

44.

I was too sick to grapple fully with Blake. I was grateful for my
friend.

45.

My memoir about my body would describe a time I tried to board a plane in another country, and they had no record of me, but the plane was about to leave and the person at the gate told me I was gorgeous, and touched my arm, and let me board, and my body was the plane and the gate and that person. And I was gorgeous.

46.

"You remember your lovers and travel," Mona Modiano, my professor of Advanced Romanticism, said. (I chose the class for its name.)

47.

Maybe she said "your lovers and travels," but I've remembered it as "travel." The final word is a command.

48.

That when my father first had cancer, at around forty, he wrote and self-published a chapbook of poems, *Crows on the Road.* One night during his final weeks he explained each line. What thou lov'st well remains.

49.

That in the first weeks of his final dying, we read the poignant texts.

And then, being so caught up in daily poignancy, its bodily flagging, we turned to texts of comedy, absurdity, joy. Beckett understood. You shit your man-diaper and take a drug and lament your grotesque swellings and go on reading. It was just like getting an MFA.

50.

I wondered what books we would have needed—after poignancy, after absurdity—if he had lived another month.

51.

Then found one, a month later, when the cancer was surely already in me, at the ancientest depths of mule elk and spruce, after doing a reading in Virginia. My wife and I woke in a friend's apartment, could have stayed for another life, snow in the air outside, could have found anything by the bed. I found Donald Revell's *Tantivy*, wept like the snow in the air outside. It answered my question. I have since found others. Have tried to write them.

52.

That certain lines I wrote before illness have become more true during it: "The dying dog could barely walk but lunged like nothing had happened." It's true, though starting to not be possible.

53.

That so many books—Beckett, etc.—were simply on the shelves of the house I grew up in. My father recommended Vonnegut and Camus when I was fourteen, and French New Wave films (he'd seen them in college, admiring fathers and sons together in the theater, then got to be that, in revival), in the same way he said exercise at that age could help some muscles most, but otherwise the books were just there. Paperbacks from a life of reading. One figure for all he offered, that larger volume.

54.

He worked in government. What is a eulogy thought: I have met renowned thinkers, scholars. Have met only a few people—and they have been my closest friends, not celebrated figures—with his ability to talk to anyone, to take an interest. When I started to publish in journals, he would read all of each issue's poems, mark the ones he liked. How many poets do that? Parenting as letting the books just be there on the shelf, which permitted. Peeing against a wall somewhere after a beer with lunch, one afternoon in New York, I'll catch up.

55.

That his working in government, his having lived, allowed me to have those books, live in a house above a floodplain on the Deschutes River, become what I am. I'd walk on the edge of the flooded fields, or past yellow grasses after flood had withdrawn. Spent most afternoons reading by the river.

56.

As a teacher, a good number of the books I mention—not that I teach but that I draw on for examples, orientations, recommend in my office—I read before I was eighteen. Most of Woolf, Duras, Baldwin, Kundera, Joyce, Calvino, Paul Auster, Jeanette Winterson, García Márquez, Emerson, Nabokov. Borges, Barth, Barthelme. Cervantes. Long before I read Cheever or Dickens or Hardy. Typical syllabus of a certain era or self. Sure, imperfect, any one thing not being everything. I speak of it and decades-old pollen returns. What exactly am I recommending?

57.

I hated high school, but the shittiness of my public, semi-rural education (I was highly graded, spent graduation among wildflowers by the river) taught me. Gave me time to actually learn. Public library education. How do you pronounce these words?

58.

A west coast story.

59.

Pacific Northwest. I didn't know about New York, didn't know until I was a professor about the distinctions among different colleges, blessedly. I swam in the river and made money chopping wood and clearing out construction sites and read.

60.

Rather than hear an elegy I think my father would like to hear what I'm reading, would like to know what the current best books are. Why do I get occupied with books that are not the best books?

61.

I was driving to a job interview when I learned he had died. I pulled over in a gas station. Then did the interview. Got the job.

62.

In those stories the hero
is beyond himself into the next
thing

CREELEY

63.

I remember that passage, like so many, with the word "already" inserted. An overtone I hear in many poems. "In those stories the hero / is *already* beyond himself." Or Yeats: "I am *already* looped in the loops of her hair." I hear it.

64.

Did I catch it from Keats? "Already with thee!" A moment that represents one peak of poetic action: as soon as he imagines the nightingale, names it, there it is, he is with it!! It makes sense this sense would run through other poems, unsaid.

65.

(voicemail from my doctor—wondering if I have any questions)

66.

(email from Michael—wondering about coming by this afternoon—I use a set of nested puns (too obscure?) to see if he has any marijuana oil/butter for baking—for nausea, please urge it on your most conservative kin, for what no sanctioned drugs can touch, it helps)

67.

I thought of the books I loved most in high school as The Literature of Longing. Wrote in a notebook at seventeen: "Write a novel called *The Literature of Longing*. Starts as an essay about *Nadja* and *Written on the Body* and *Giovanni's Room* and becomes a novel in a related style? Set it in Paris?"

68.

A year later, I stopped using question marks in my notebooks. Set it in Paris.

69.

That I'd been enthralled by Annie Dillard's *Living by Fiction*. Got it from the library because of the title. Focuses on writers Dillard calls "contemporary modernists." Uses that term because it's deliberately unwieldly, won't become jargon, a brand, lose complexity. I loved that choice. I think of it whenever I see someone whose main goal seems to be to advance jargon, a brand, lose complexity.

61.

Could you name your literary movement something no one will remember except when they are reading about it. If you believe strongly enough in reading. Someone is speaking against "quietude" but I am quietly listening.

62.

Dillard's book is about writers of what's more commonly called "metafiction" (is it still?). Thesis: that metafiction—with its self-consciousness, digressions, laying bare of conventions, intricate artistry, innovation, indulgences, confoundings—was developmentally useful for me in high school. Moreso than whatever we were assigned in high school. Because adolescence is a metafictional experience (witnessing oneself constructing one's character and story, I mean witnessing myself, reveling in the potential and multiplicity of construction, finding the story we are in). (It is appropriate that at this point in the text, I see I have numbered the sections incorrectly, a minor way to get more from a form.)

63.

In *The Literature of Longing*, there is no plot except desire. Or, rather, there is no plot except for desire's desire to be a sufficient plot.

64.

Setting can be limited to a bedroom or a car parked where no one can see. My girlfriend and I parked where no one could see. She said, "People say sharing a sense of humor matters. Sharing a sense of beauty matters more." We debated open-eyed vs. close-eyed kissing, without yet kissing. When you close your eyes, are you turning inward, toward the experience, or away from it, away from the actual other? I was thinking, "What about a novel with no plot except looking into another's eyes?" It is possible I knew little (cared little) about plot.

65.

You might read David Foster Wallace saying that reading John Barth's metafiction is like getting laid by someone who keeps interrupting the fucking to say, "Here I am, laying you."

66.

As though that isn't sexy. ("Fuck me slower then come on my back," my beautiful friend said. And looked in my eyes: "There you are.")

67.

Or you might note that John Barth's *Lost in the Funhouse* was first published in 1968 and think (a) its methods of experiment still seem interesting, more exciting than many recent books, even ones widely celebrated for certain types of experiment, so have those authors read it? If so, whatever their relationship is to that particular book, have they contended with the lineage and ambitions of "contemporary modernism" in a sophisticated and principled way, or is it true that contemporary "literary fiction" is mostly a commercial genre, one that is often actively anti-artistic and apolitical and psychologically retrograde and less deftly written than fiction in other genres, just another object of cultural production? And (b) the time between 1968 and 2015 is roughly equivalent to the time between 1968 and 1922, when *Ulysses* was published. If the line from *Ulysses* to *Funhouse* is clear. What do you want to do tonight.

68.

Or you might read this famous passage from *Lost in the Funhouse* sitting by a river, like I did:

"He wishes he had never entered the funhouse. But he has. Then he wishes he were dead. But he's not. Therefore he will construct funhouses for others and be their secret operator—though he would rather be among the lovers for whom funhouses are designed."

69.

But I don't know if there are any secrets, at least not after we've met each other.

70.

When I first went to Paris, a bit after imagining setting a novel there (I will never write a novel, wouldn't write a novel for my life), I planned to cultivate noble, brooding isolation by reading *The Brothers Karamazov*, be a severe hermit. But on my first night, reading at a bar, somebody asked me what I was reading, and invited me somewhere, where I met some Corsican magicians, and I never read a word. It is possible I have never read a word. (That there were years in my life when I could sit at a bar, reading, until someone invited me somewhere, and I wanted it, and went.)

71.

My course on The Literature of Longing would include the moment
in Canto V of Dante's *Inferno* when the lovers abandon the pretense
of reading ("That day we read no more") and the moment with a
woman I met when I was sitting at a bar reading (she asked if I wanted some of the bread from her plate), who had a copy of the *Inferno*
from the public library in her car, and I read her that passage, and then
we read no more.

72.

Half an hour later, in the parking lot of an apartment complex (she'd
taken me to see a tree she liked). A sudden battering. Woman at the
windshield. Help I woke up he was hitting me he has a gun he's coming
back. We stood with her for a long time under a tree, waiting for the
police. Holding hands. The three of us.

73.

I thought: if he returns, with a gun, anything, and this is the end, all
right, this is where we are, an end.

74.

She asked how I'd known to do that. To stand under a tree. Holding hands.

75.

She protested, after everything, when I praised her body: "You should've seen me when I was twenty-two. My body would've killed you."

76.

That I rose twice in the night to frolic and calm myself in the bathroom, so aroused by sleeping near her, her dog's tongue under the door.

77.

She woke and said is there anything I can do to make you instantly hard again. Googled sunrise and said that was my deadline. Things worked out well enough. For a while I thought of her saying "is there anything I can do" and that was well enough.

78.

It's tempting to continue to recall, indulge, inappropriate someone will say but also my life (I don't care to be beyond critique, I am not a thesis I am proving, we have been here and here again, imperfectly): someone else, touching the front of my shirt, like it was something further than fabric. Who then went and changed where I could see. I was young enough to apologize for seeing her—it was clearly what she wanted. She looked at me with no ruse.

79.

Or fucking a girlfriend facing the mirror. Her hand on the mirror. Below a handprint from some days ago, when we had fucked facing the mirror. This funhouse, a world.

80.

That I too have been written about. In an autobiographical novel, for example. A woman I dated for a month. In her story it is a few months, but it was a month. I learn she blamed the man inordinately when she told her friends about the breakup, for the sake of story or her own pain or a moment's saleable insight. And suddenly I understood a chill that became part of my life, which I experienced at the time as life's chill, existential due, and why a few years later, at a party with a person I'd been dating for three years, someone pulled her aside and said honey you should avoid him, he hurts women. I question myself still, remembering.

81.

Must there be occasion for every grief of our childhood before we are done, asks Merwin.

82.

That in my memory I ended the relationship when it was clear the surge of its first weeks had weakened for me, deepened for her. Dating meant making such decisions, offering such hurt, hurting oneself, even.

83.

I didn't know how to talk to her about how I didn't know how to talk
to her, feels like the main thing now, partly because I had never known
someone from her background (wealthy, Ivy League, confident in connections, at least to my seeing, then), or—who turned experience into
stories as though there were no question of being a main character, able
narrator, no question of the narration of one's life and one's problems
mattering as a topic, or, even if those were questions—those questions
were one's to ask and analyze. How can I say this except unfairly.

84.

Don't be so quiet, she would say after analyzing something from her
past. Or: I don't need another impassive man in my life (referring to
her father). I didn't understand anything and responded as I did: bom-
bastic, quiet. Also, was hapless, overly lyrical, generally ill-equipped,
twenty-two, inarticulate, overwhelmed by someone who started so
many sentences by saying, "I will say." I did not have a comparable
phrase (or will) with which to begin.

85.

Kissing and telling? Trying that as a route, on this precipice. Typical,
petty: a life.

86.

"But in the end one tires of the high-flown," begins Merrill's "About the Phoenix." Go on:

Ah, how well one might,
If it were less than a matter of life or death,
Traffic in strong prescriptions, "live" and "die"!
But couldn't the point about the phoenix
Be not agony or resurrection, rather
A mortal lull that followed either

87.

That my beautiful friend seems to be going to Istanbul, my wife to Cairo. I want them to travel to these places, would feel sorrowful but not betrayed if they never return, assuming the travel, staying, upheld and advanced what one would ever care about making exist in a relationship. The reasons for loving in the first place.

88.

If in a future year we will all be on a patio. Or separate patios, or alone, in variable combinations. What will we not be grateful for, what won't seem like mercy, being there.

89.

The obligation of the possible. "There can't be too much love," my
wife has advised.

90.

The fortune of romantic complications, the energy to have them, in a
country that won't put you to death for following them, in all our brief
unknowing.

91.

Early on, I sent my wife Cavafy's "Half an Hour." He describes
talking, drunk, with a person in a bar. "I never had you, nor I suppose
/ will I ever have you," he begins (trans. Keeley/Sherrard), describing
"half an hour that was totally erotic." Goes on:

And I think you understood this
and stayed slightly longer on purpose.
That was very necessary.

92.

"That was very necessary." Such mercy in that, more intimate than a tryst.
Compare this poem's vision of the imagination to Michaux's in "Cries."

93.

Cavafy, I sometimes say in a class. A poet of—you know that moment when you are sharing an armrest, very aware of the armrest?

94.

Early on, she took me to the bird sanctuary and recited Yeats.

95.

Before that: she appeared, climbed on my lap in golden light while I sat at the kitchen table. We walked into town (this is Amherst), crossing railroad tracks I crossed daily that year. How distinct: of all the crossings, that one.

96.

I was a mess, trying to "make it work" with someone else, telling myself life was suffering, for the long haul, doing the right thing, falling apart, on the verge of self-blaming therapy or marrying to swallow deeper and she said maybe the problem is you aren't with me, and then I was, and it has been easy (despite deaths, illnesses, living together in a lonely town for a while, economy, war, daily humiliations, aging) ever since.

97.

I told my father as he was dying, with more humility than hubris: that though I was sure my wife and I would suffer in many ways, unknowably, horribly, there were types of suffering we would not need to know, because of each other, and others we would need to, we understood, from the fortune. (If I imagine myself waking into myself at twelve, all this life only a vision, with the knowledge I have now and the chance to live again: I would study poetry at the University of Washington, and I would look for her.)

98.

That when we decided to marry I saw us walking across railroad tracks in golden light toward what I understood was equally death and the rest of all of life, beyond us, it has happened very soon and continually ever since.

99.

I wish to God I had made this world, this scurvy
And disastrous place

WRIGHT

100.

heroic in its ordinariness,
the slow-picked, halting traverse of a pitch
where the fiercest attention becomes routine
—look at the faces of those who have chosen it.

RICH

1.

Oh but somebody (yawn) is asking if poetry matters. (Poetry is matter.) Better to ask why you would ask poetry to justify itself, though it has existed everywhere. What does this question say about our shame, alienation from things that have existed everywhere? Our suspicion of them? What does it suggest about all that we do not ask to justify itself?

2.

And how does this suspicion of poetry make us susceptible to compensatory justifications: justifying poetry by a theory, a scene, reduced rhetorical or commercial meanings, anything other than its experiential fact, its necessary agitations (alleviation is a form of agitation). As with those who'd justify arts education by narrow vocational functions. They've already lost.

3.

Justify why you have an eye. How come nursery rhymes, how come tulips and clouds, fear and bread, insight without immediate application. What is the vocational justification for mud.

4.

So I made the following syllabus:

The names of the successive hours of centuries may have ostensible
names, but the name of each of them is one of the singers,

The name of each is, eye-singer, ear-singer, head-singer,
sweet-singer, night-singer, parlor-singer, love-singer, weird-singer,
or something else.

WHITMAN

5.

Write a poem as one of the singers and then as all of them.

6.

That for days I have woken with a phrase from Agha Shahid Ali
lighting the slowly lighting room: "Hurt into memory." Compare to
Dickinson: "Remorse—Is memory—Awake." Or Richard Wilbur,
on waking: "The soul shrinks // From all that it is about to remember." Langston Hughes: "I don't dare start thinking in the morning."
Alice Notley: "The goal of awakening is black coffee."

7.

Don't start a story with a character waking, you have advised. But
this is not a story, and if it is it has started already, long before I find
myself in the room with a gold and red scarf for curtains.

8.

(doctor calls again—says we will address this quickly—either operate
immediately or figure another treatment, then operate—he has
consulted a team—gives me his personal cell—says don't call after 10
PM unless I need to)

9.

(Michael comes by—interpreted my fishing for weed-infused baking
ingredients as a request for olive oil and butter—brings them, ordinary miracle—and with him in the kitchen—suddenly I remember
an echo of Ali's phrase, from Auden—"Mad Ireland hurt you into
poetry"—why don't people quote that line of the stanza, or the final
lines—"It survives, / a way of happening, a mouth"—more than "Poetry makes nothing happen"—clearly this is a complicated nothing,
which happens to one—hurts us into—survives—but people like the
dumber line, dumber interpretation—it serves our apologetic fears)

10.

The first poem I memorized was "The Secret Garden" by Rita Dove.
It starts:

I was ill, lying on my bed of old papers
when you came with white rabbits in your arms;
and the doves scattered upwards, flying to mothers

I know I am a poet because it was only now, fourteen years later, that it occurs to me that "doves" could be seen as a reference to the author. I've always taken the word at its word.

11.

The doves in the poem have always been doves, not symbols. The white rabbits are white rabbits. The arms, arms. I don't know if this is the correct way to read, but it is the way I read. Each metaphor is (more than) actual.

12.

Because what does light rain mean? What does waking early and memorizing poetry mean? What does even the clearest statement mean— "I love my friends." But that takes a life to understand.

13.

"There are times when reality comes closer" (Roethke). "It was like / A new knowledge of reality" (Stevens). Of course the imagination is political.

14.

I memorized those lines on Seattle buses. Wasn't there a single bus that would take me to my internship faster? But I wouldn't have seen so much of the city. Wouldn't have met the man who told me "no one but your parents will suffer for you" then pulled down his pants so I could see a live scar.

15.

Wouldn't have met the blind man who could still see periwinkle. Had a piece of paper the right color. If you wrote letters with your finger, just right, he could spell by the moving shade. (There's a poetry thought here: to be able to be next to him, spelling like that, I had to already be speaking with him; but the writing mattered, was matter.) Also Stevens, from that year (of course this line was written when I first read it, in 2002, and it has been written newly again every year it has been read, not only in the year it was written): "The world must be measured by eye."

16.

"Yet once more," starts Milton. "Always for the first time" (Breton). "Each will astonish you" (Levertov, speaking of subsequent seasons—I have not found a truer statement). "As for we who 'love to be astonished'" (Hejinian). What *else* does poetry need to be accountable to? Syllabus: now, for the first time in history, write a poem that starts.

17.

Hurt into memory. In Iowa City, in the seventh month of winter,
I read an interview with James Merrill, in a coffee shop named
with an unfortunate pun (he would have enjoyed it: Grounds for
Dessert—as though instead of cake, you'd get old coffee grounds,
a reason to leave). I went there because no one else did. Where
I read all of Mackey, all of Williams (a period I was doing that).
Merrill described revising a line from "the morning was worse" to
"the morning was better," something like that, because, he said, the
first version was all posture. Really, mornings are better. (Which
isn't always true, but I see what he means.)

18.

The sun will come up. Tomorrow, tomorrow, and tomorrow or the
next day.

19.

I read Merrill all that winter, arriving an hour early at the community college where I taught, sitting in the student union's small café
to watch snow and read. I'd teach three composition classes, im-
provising a lesson plan in the first, delivering it well in the second,
too closely hurrying in the third. I often just brought in poems,
including that one by Ali, "Snow in the Desert."

20.

The title of the poem is "Snow on the Desert," not "in," but I prefer
how I remember it.

21.

The phrase I remember does not appear in the poem, not exactly.
Instead: "the rays hurting each cactus // into memory" and "the
past now happening so quickly that each // stoplight hurts us
into memory" and "I remembered // another moment that refers
only to itself." One isn't hurt into specific recollection, when hurt
into memory, the bark of today's dog recalling yesterday's bite.
But is transubstantiated into molecules of memory itself—we,
like each cactus, each stoplight, come to compose an instant, even
this one, that is already too far beyond us to comprehend. Here
we are. Can you remember that.

22.

Before a friend's wedding, Brooklyn. My wife and I have a drink at
a rosy bar, on a narrow bench out front, backs against stained glass,
iron railing pressing our knees. Exhausted from travel into the city,
though I can't tell you how we got there—bus? train? from where?
But I know we were there and for several minutes I understood we
were minor figures in a painting, features smudged. The painting of

our lives would stay on a gallery wall long after we had faded, and the bicycles passing had, and the herbs in my cocktail which must have been in fashion, whatever century this was.

23.

To become a trace, in Pound's sense: "Nothing matters but the quality / of the affection— / in the end—that has carved the trace in the mind / dove sta memoria."

24.

And to become a trace in the sense in which Pound did, while writing *The Pisan Cantos*. Caged, awaiting a verdict on his treason, humbled (crazed), achieving, in his regret, his distemper, instances of delicacy that may be one of the closest records there is of something like redemption on earth, however partial, implicated, horrific, generic, flawed (would it be redemption if it demanded purity?): "as live wind in the beech grove / as strong air amid cypress." "The olives grey over grey holding walls."

25.

To have believed in poetry enough to bring a section of *The Pisan Cantos* to my composition classes at the community college. To have explained that certain lines lean forward and back simultaneously, ardently chalking the prosody. To say, as though a scholar from another era, as though I'd read everything, that Pound wrote more beautiful lines than anyone since Chaucer, even if his poems do not cohere, much as paradise is present, he says, "apparently only in fragments." Why did I think—and when did I stop thinking—this was sufficient pedagogy? My students listened, smiled, gave good evaluations, learned who knows what, but something, something, they must have.

26.

When I first taught Beginning Poetry, we did other experiments. One day, I had everyone spend ten minutes staring quietly into a partner's eyes. Then they read Robert Duncan's "Often I Am Permitted to Return to a Meadow" in unison and wrote a poem.

27.

But then, after I first memorized that first poem, someone told me Rita Dove wasn't the right poet to be reading. Maybe it was the guy who hung out at Café Allegro in a cardigan, who told me he was writing a paper about how authors are influenced by authors born after them? That, he said, would be the future of all literary criticism.

28.

So I found H.D. saying something similar:

I would forego
my snowfields for your sun,
I would surrender
crocus
and ice-gentian
and all the lilies
rising one by one,
one after one,
and then another one

Was H.D. the right poet to be reading?

29.

Where else have I seen that flower? (I have seen most flowers
in poems.) Oh, in Emily Dickinson! "The Gentian weaves her
fringes." Which takes me to James Schuyler: "Is it stamina / that
unseasonably freaks / forth a bluet?" You learn a new name for a
flower. You see it everywhere. I would tell my friend in the cardigan now—what need for literary criticism, with these lines, these
associations? (There's that cadence from Roethke again, my mind
is mostly made up.)

30.

John and I sat at the Café Allegro and read Whitman. Very good
almond croissants. We asked the book questions and opened to any

page. Or we walked around the Pike Place Market speaking only in questions, then only in verbs, only in prepositions. We read our poems to ducks and made revisions based on their counsel.

31.

Revision means re-seeing, no one should ever say again except as something obvious everyone knows or can gather in a glance. Ditto "essay means to try" (required to say in most books of lyrical prose). "Stanza means room." "Poetry makes nothing happen." Go to your stanza.

32.

That I recently received a rejection from a Big Magazine. "These poems are <u>superb</u>," the editor wrote, "but superb in a more postmodern sense than we usually like, to be quite honest."

33.

"These pies are <u>superb</u>," the judge of the pie contest said, "but superb in a more pie-modern pie than we usually pie, to be pie honest." "I'm not interested in recent pies," said the professor-baker.

34.

Can poetry be taught they asked me at dinner. Better to ask what is poetry especially good at teaching, I muttered to the departmentally funded prawns. ("How do you know about so many recent books," one poet-professor asked me in the bathroom. I think he was teaching a version, a version, only a version of poetry, I think a version reflecting more about his own academic ambition and anxiety than any urge toward the complicated, impossible, full-throated whole. How can he face the dead.)

35.

You need to keep correcting things, which is also an illness response, to rail where one can, given all that can't be argued with. Like, there's the notion that "easier" poems are better for certain populations. Children, the incarcerated, retirees, etc. How patronizing, insulting to people and art. I assure you people anywhere can read and respond to anything you offer. Even Mary Karr, whose views about poetry I often find hilarious, affirms it, in one of her hilarious memoirs. And Kenneth Koch on reading Donne to eight-year-olds and asking them to write and the results will get you further into Donne than a buncha dogged term papers. Poets apologize for poetry so quickly, why? Bring anyone the good stuff, what are you saving it for? As though certain populations can eat only fast food, as though thought doesn't expand as fast as language can, if you'll let it. Better to say poetry is not fabricated for an audience but grants audience. Shakespeare was also a child.

36.

When I taught poetry and photography at the American Indian reservation on the Washington coast, a ten-year-old wrote, in response to Stein:

Pencil in a nencil.
Pencil, what's a nencil?

37.

What need for literary criticism? Her couplet is syllabus enough. Language generates/enters/expands the known/unknown, via a poetic technique, sound of the word pencil calling forth the nencil. Then asks itself about it (through the sound of pencil on the page). Not what does "nencil" *mean*. But what is it. One writes to find out what is it.

38.

Diving makes the water deep.

39.

That talking about poetry can feel like rinsing soup. Dickinson: "They shut me up in Prose." Keats: "It is easier to think what Poetry should be than to write it." (He says this in preference for the actual, not as a dissembling via negativa, à la some recent facile deconstructionism of certain critics, which claims actual poetry is chiefly of value for the impossible ideals it invokes and fails to achieve, as though

the value of a friend is in how they fail to be every other friend or
an Ideal friend or this meal is better when it's pure potential, or
even better when it's undercooked and thus brings to mind a better
version, and some toothsome bile, rather than a specific tomato with
basil in your mouth. Especially if you're hungry, the meal is better
in your mouth, the actual meal, the actual friend at your table, the
imperfect sun in your eyes, the millions of suns that Whitman knew
are left are real, he identified them, didn't imagine them, le Paradise
n'est pas artificiel but spezzato, and stranger.)

40.

That talking about poetry can feel like there's this drug that will fuck
up your own personal liver, so you feed it to a horse (prose) and drink
the (poetics) urine. The horse does not survive. (Poet, step away from
that horse.)

41.

Jay emails from Seattle:

"Well, your note (wrote 'night' first!) and this cup of coffee kept me
from swatting myself back into my paid-work where I 'ought' to be
as Finn is off IDing ferns in Seward Park with Alex ('swowd foon!')
and I'm also dealing with gutter guy, weedwhacker repair guy, etc.,
and last night's weird dead blankly-menacing humidity broke into a
big red sunset and this crisp sea-salty morning. Still hot. Cait's out of

town—taking a test in LA with actors paid to fake medical problems which C is challenged to diagnose—so I'm otherwise always with Finn. 'Cucumber moon!,' he shouted three nights ago in that Yeatsy 'trembling blue-green' evening. 'Man onna moon poop inna sock?,' he asked the last time I changed his diaper. 'Axolot!' he shouted when he saw one in a book. So I guess this indicates, if I also tell you I'm reading Bartone's book Paul's Romans Ch7/8 (all creation is groaning) Pound's Classic Anthology and Helen Keller writing about how it feels to be deaf and blind, where my head is at."

42.

I'm looking at a picture of us in Texas, a decade ago. He looks beautiful in a sweater vest and I am laughing at anything.

43.

That a colleague has started giving me his books. Zukofsky's *A*, knotty critical works, some of Pound's more obscure translations. It seems he's keeping the more lyrical volumes for his shelves. I tell him, oh, Pound can be sweepingly lyrical, too, and I quote some lines. Having read much of Pound to find those lines. I would rather now discuss them with my friend.

44.

I would rather talk to him than read, in part, because the memory

I'm hurt into is of the present, in which I often find beauty painful to behold, that it should exist, its affront, despite all this, world
and its conditions, and mine, leading where. Hard to imagine
devoting hours now to reading the pages I would need to, to find
more lines to recite. I am left with what I have, typical as it is.
Perhaps the issue is that illness is an inherently lyrical state,
in what it does to a self and time, in how it removes one from
the striving world, so what need for poetry? Yeats: "Maybe at last
being but a broken man / I must be satisfied with my heart."

45.

I never wanted literature, to read or write, not exactly. I wanted
the life it has taught me to see. And now? Carl Phillips: "The way
art can become, eventually, all we have / of what was true." Which
I used to hear as an ambition, not a lament: to become only art.

46.

When my father first had cancer, he wrote a draft of a novel.
It included a character who was writing a novel while a lake
destroyed the resort he owned. In the end he throws his novel
into the lake, lets the resort crumble, returns to his wife. I have
spent my life trying to write a book that is worth throwing into
such a lake.

47.

I wrote about it in one of the first pieces I published, a short essay in the *Seneca Review*. I wrote, in 2004, what I understand now is the first draft of this book:

Crumbling Expectations

I stood behind the counter ringing the bell for myself. My father had cancer and wrote two drafts of a novel called *Crumbling Expectations* about a Lake Michigan resort owner whose resort falls into the lake. I spent my childhood in Michigan and remember going to the resort. My father told me that boatsmen prefer oceans to the Great Lakes, and that some spots have ice all summer. The resort owner tries everything to save his resort, while neglecting his marriage (and having an affair in the barn loft) and destroying old social/business relationships (and his relationships with his aging regulars). I remember my mom saying the sex scene might be too much for me. My dad said I had read worse. (I read from my parents' shelves. I often think that I will never be as smart as when I had read only those books.) It was colon cancer. In the last scene, the resort crumbles into the lake and the exhausted resort owner, letting it go, embraces his wife. I saw this as a metaphor for the novel: my father abandoned it, healed from surgery and chemo, embraced his wife. That is, the book defeats itself for the things that make books worth having. I thought this thought and, as it were, crumbled into a lake: I tried to write myself into the story—I tried to talk myself into it, the idiom would go, as I had decided that talking to myself was the best way to learn to be a writer. Language existed, unendingly, one just had to join it. (I despised Auden with his "if I could tell you I would let you know." I could tell you.) (When I told the first teacher I respected that I couldn't articulate anything, he told me that I could "articulate like a motherfucker" and had other problems.) I walked along the river with the book under my arm. The river was below our development, you knew it by the lining of trees. I put myself at the counter, put the story in Washington state, and rang the bell for myself. [I excise here a passage of metafiction, which culminates with my story-within-a-story's-story self discovering a manuscript.] My father's father died when my father was young, as did his father. Two years ago, in New York, my dad and I shared a hotel room. The shower curtain had a strong plastic smell. During chemotherapy, he said, he couldn't take that smell. I remember being embarrassed by the weight he gained, the hair he lost. When I overheard my grandmother say he had told her there was beauty everywhere, even in winter, I thought she was talking about me. I don't think he ever told me there is beauty everywhere, but he was reading a book by one of my teachers, and he marked his page with a matchstick, and he set his water glass by the bed. I jerked off later thinking of a character in a Paul Auster novel from his shelf who jerks off in a hotel room while his mentor sleeps. I didn't realize a book is itself an embrace. I quote back to my father now words he has written but never wrote.

48.

The book entering the water—equivalent to the quality of the affection that carves a trace in the mind.

49.

That, beauty being painful to behold, I stay up watching action movies. Let there be Russian roulette in the pre-credits. Then the hero, a broken man, is avoiding memories by drinking. He's at a liquor store, counting coins for the cheapest liter, when wannabe robbers burst in, you wanna make trouble broken man, shut up! But he remembers— no, he can't NOT remember—his training in the application of pain, blammo! The baddies go down. Store's owner is like just take the bottle. He drinks staggering home.

50.

"Let me explain. When I'm sober. When I'm healthy and well. I hurt people. I drink to weaken the machine they made," says one broken hero in his ending speech, explaining to his girl how come after he got all the revenge he immediately went to shit again. (We love us our trauma heroes, easier than hating all that causes trauma, or imagining ways of experiencing experience that are as full as trauma and of trauma yet not trauma exactly, or that imagine trauma as something other than a personal affliction/obstacle/attribute? So that the goal isn't a tale of individual triumph but shared seeing, being in it? Hugo, on a ruined town: "I was desolate, too, and so survived.")

51.

You've read so many memoirs about people stopping drinking, it has sometimes felt like why would you need to? You already know what it would be like.

52.

You've drunk enough in some far-ago seasons to have considered it stopping drinking to not add whiskey to your coffee in the morning, or to start the day with beer instead of whiskey, or to sober up at the night's end with a bottle of white wine instead of gin and whatever, or to not feel anxious if there's less than a bottle per person at the party.

53.

Equally reasonable response to my specific illness: drink as much as I can while I can, light the dance floor's lanterns with hundred dollar bills, assassinate some lobbyists, drive all the cars.

54.

I may not know what is reasonable.

55.

The phrase appeals to me—hurt into memory—because it seems better than having memory lead to hurt, preserving it. (How much of this view is generational? I remember hating how Bush's response to September 11th required holding onto a mythic and infantilized idea of the US's innocence, in order to support his version of the assault. I remember hating most his saying "you are either with us or against us," feeling comforted, in Europe, by graffiti responding "Bush: neither nor." It is hard for me to imagine phrasing almost anything in terms of "with us or against us," whatever the cause; I do not know if this is correct. I suppose I think about poetry as I do because of this.) But when hurt into memory. The child cries and there's the world.

56.

Edgar's curse in *King Lear*, the most affecting I know: "O world." Every poem an extension. Each will astonish you.

57.

Edgar, who flees his birthright, responsibilities, feigning madness. Until he meets the actually mad king. For whom suffering is not liberty but frustration, choicelessness, fear. Poets who prefer to be Edgar on the heath.

58.

Jay's letter is better than most essays about poetry. Let's say because it offers *inductive poetics* rather than *deductive poetics*. This is a distinction I have invented just now and won't ever mention again. *Deductive poetics* precede from premises. E.g., you might have a premise like you don't like postmodern poetry, no matter how <u>superb</u> it is. Or that a poem should primarily demonstrate/engage with/counter a particular theory or be pleasing to a particular scene or advance your own or someone else's celebrity. You then write and read and evaluate and discuss poems—that is, you arrive at varied *experiences* of poetry—in relation to those premises. *Inductive poetics* precede from experience. Language is experiential. La la. Yum. You then write and read and evaluate and discuss poems—that is, you arrive at varied *premises* about poetry—in relation to those experiences. These results might contradict. Brilliant!

59.

"I wanted the work to show the process of composition," a poet told me recently, as though any work doesn't, as though cracks don't appear in each loaf, as though you can build a perfect birdhouse. He is reverent to that premise. It absolves him.

60.

As though Shakespeare or whoever didn't know language is material and word/world conflict and the self is multiple and performed and also real and sound rushes ahead of sense in revealing yet reorienting ways within a manner of speaking in a place and time, but these are minor points, or starting points, not sufficient conclusions to be pious toward. Hopkins and Herbert as religious poets of inductive poetics, compared to the deductive religious poets of dogma or the deductive experimental or proudly conservative poets of dogma. Predictable types of sounds come from the audience in response and they leave affirmed. (What Frost says about modern poetry being of subtraction, not addition: I read a book in which every line is a certain kind of pun, isolated technique, one gummy bear in the test tube, but where are the real bears?)

61.

That I'm trying to read poems instead of reading what people are saying about poetry online, the commentary and corrections, media cycles of instant response and what do we agree we all hate today (I am thinking about a particular spat, will not record it). I find there is usually more in the poems. So I pick up *Lovers in the Used World* by Gillian Conoley. The book's title is poem (and poetics) enough. When its title is no longer poem and poetics enough, you can read the title of the first poem:

"The World"

Then its first phrase:

"It was just a gas station."

The title and first phrase are poem and poetics enough.

62.

I emailed T—— about it:

"Epiphany is fine, but more than wisdom, maybe one wants the
posture that comes after, which, given time, I suppose also means
comes before. I love the hugeness of the poem's title, of the initial
'it.' How 'just' doesn't deflate magnitude but retains it—renders it, in
every sense—offering 'just' proportion. It has the quality of 'common
everyday inevitability' you mentioned a while ago, a gorgeous phrase.
The real epiphany is another moment."

63.

I continued (I was excited, I couldn't sleep, wish to indulge this
while I can):

"Anyhow, I know, I know, such a posture might seem nonchalant
or diffident, or even to valorize disavowal, preferring the aftermath
to the precise thick of it, but I'm increasingly desirous of/trusting
in (I mean those words the same? to trust is to desire?) its qualities
of spanking, focused ease, which are far from simple. Reminds me
of Creeley's 'Envoi'—do you know it? Gleefully dismantles the

premises of creative writing pedagogy:

Particulars they want,
particulars they
fucking well will

get, love. For openers,
you—the stars
earth revolves about

"Which sounds reckless, defiant, but also is a mode of restraint and even more difficult REVERENCE: insisting that '*you*' is a sufficient particular, equivalent to multiple stars, and thus there must be multiple earths, or zagging pinball earths, in relation to them. There's restraint, in the opening, but also hurtling. Sense of crashing into a landscape and then pausing there. Is this a meadow? You find a clearing, apparent lack, so you can see what's moving in it—this is pure Whitman? Has both careening and care, I think. Reminds me of a line from your book, one I think of often: 'with some coaxing they move on their stilts'—the stilts are already on!! I love that tenderness, the coaxing is itself acrobatic…"

64.

But I can't shake that thought about deductive and inductive poetics. Jay mentioned Pound, and I keep mentioning Pound, and I mentioned religion, so I'm reminded of Pound's speculation about religion in *The Spirit of Romance*:

"There are, as we see, only two kinds of religion. [The type] where someone, having to keep a troublesome rabble in order, invents and scares them with a disagreeable bogie, which he calls god.

"…forms of ecstatic religion, on the other hand, are not in inception dogma or propaganda of something called the *one truth* or the *universal truth*; they *seem* little concerned with ethics; their general object appears to be to stimulate a sort of confidence in the life-force. Their teaching is variously and constantly a sort of working hypothesis acceptable to people of a certain range of temperament—a 'regola' which suits a particular constitution of nerves and intellect.… One must consider that the types which joined these cults survived, in Provence, and survive, today—priests, maenads and the rest—though there is in our society no provision for them."

65.

I spend more time with *The Spirit of Romance*. I could still feel nostalgic for a time when a critical move was to perform a "who would win" on Shakespeare vs. Dante. Have I mentioned the best image in all of poetry? Elizabeth Bishop, somewhere in her letters, identifies the best image in all of poetry. The best image in all of poetry, I believe she says, is the end of W.H. Auden's "The Fall of Rome":

Altogether elsewhere, vast

Herds of reindeer move across
Miles and miles of golden moss,
Silently and very fast.

66.

That's what I mean about correctives vs. what's correct (yes who can
say what is correct yes it varies and changes and the meanings do we
can't say it perfectly yes yes but we say something true for now try
to you know when you are trying to it is possible or listen until we
hear). It is a good corrective to say we shouldn't be concerned with
canonical "who would wins" or identifying the best. But I'd like to
read those essays, aware they will be partial, absurd, circumstantial—
what's wrong with the partial, with what we are partial to? I mention
this, ridiculously ventingly, to some friends in a reply-all. They pick
up on the question about the best image.

Jordan says:

"Reading all over, in no real order, parts of Robert Graves' *The White
Goddess*. I'm sure all of you combined, or even alone, would add so
much to what's already in this book about perhaps one of the earliest
and most powerful images in the Western world. I read about Keats
seeing her, a combination of love, death from consumption, and
poetry, and how, when she leaves, she leaves him 'Alone and palely
loitering.' I know you said to keep quiet about the BEST, which I
can do, since today it's picturing Keats all a mess, unable to marry

Fanny Brawn for so many reasons, and then does entering the poem ('Belle Dame Sans Merci') almost turn poetry itself into that one final unreach for him? …but then I read 'the close connection of winds with the Goddess is also shown in the widespread popular belief that only pigs and goats (both anciently sacred to her) can see the wind, and the belief that mares can conceive merely by turning thire hindquarters to the wind,' and this is now the image, today, that alives me again. All this during coffee, then, later to the pool with the kids. Yesterday it was goats and bison, fishing with bamboo rods with corn bait, and they catch 5 bluegill but afraid to toss them back, so I did, and feeling my hands get that fish itch from the sharp poke of some part of the fins."

Melissa says:

"Momentarily I'm thinking of what needs to be painted and what needs to be packed and maybe there is some poetic value in the image of the soggy cornflakes on the floor?"

Kaethe says:

"Outside the window the Lost River isn't open yet but red lifeguards putter over foot bridges made of faux rock and fountains make ejaculatory protests from the wading pools. The hallways of Glacier Canyon lodge are endless, the carpet end-stopped with moose. The older child says she is going to bed with her boyfriend and her husband. The younger child shrieks and shrieks and that makes his roseola rash brighter. My father is wearing a swimming suit that actually seems to be knee-length biking shorts.

"I haven't read a whole book of poetry for a long time. My town puts little poems on the sidewalk, though. Like in Iowa City except the poets are not-famous and the poems sometimes not-good. Mine should be stamped in cement sometime in August."

And you want me to read literary criticism? You want me to believe that life is foregone, merely theoretical, that this week's cheesiest online click-bait poetry debates and social calibrations matter more than how words move fully in these full lives? (I do not record the specific debate, there are some I celebrate...) Or that poetry should aspire to something TV or newspaper editorials or other forms do better, no matter how much of life and language that leaves out, rather than...

67.

Increasingly feeling...

One can't overstate the value of continual insistence...

On art's values, its terms and values...

Which include questions of how meaning is made, is harder than what we know...

And that is the work of poetry…

To have a thing that exists by such insistence…

Says a lot about what surrounds it…

What lets it continue existing, such a tendril…

What need for heaven…

68.

I haven't mentioned my pain in a bit, keep taking pills, trying not to think about the next tests. "Pity me," the troubadour cries. And then? One is pitied and remains equally piteous.

69.

At the end of the film the broken man speaks to whoever is left and keeps talking, longer than he should, inevitably, as Beckett knew.

70.

I've realized that this essay, loosely about poetics, in favor of looseness about poetics, is really an essay about friendship. I would care most to talk about poetry as a way of talking with a friend. Deductive/inductive—wouldn't it be better if we were in a kitchen? You could help me care or not.

71.

So I wrote Tyler:

"Boss—Working on a prose piece that is maybe going into a quick section on friendship and poetry. Remember when we taught that brief course to teens at Kenyon? Which I called Happy Poet Friends and you called Happy Poetry Friends, which small difference says a lot about the comradely propulsion we wanted? Do you remember what we taught in it? Maybe I'll fold your answer into the essay, essay as a furthering of that course… xo, Z"

And received immediately:

"Friend: I remember asking them to take walks together, a la *Ten Walks/Two Talks*, I remember asking them to write a poem that transacted in the conveyable magic of befriending another poem, and I remember asking them to write an epistle in the mode of Hugo on a barstool or predawn fishing boat. The particular pleasures of the first being the walk and documentation, Oppenesque in the mode of 'all this is reportage': isn't it always? A daybook? Always a traveler's sensibility, a traveler's experience? How this thrilled our writers into possibility; how (I think?) we made them walk with someone they didn't know and so the recorded conversation was the process of strange becoming familiar, or sometimes staying strange, etc., what it was like to begin to discover someone in words, that intimacy, what it was like for all the rest of us to witness this act performing itself, etc. An exercise to convey the basic modes, those walks then became a syllabus and rubric for the rest of what we were doing in the class. Then the exercise to write a poem that befriended another poem— how I thrilled to this—as a basic response to creative work we love— the response poem saying to the original poem 'I want to find a way to befriend you, to be more intimate with you, to become more vulnerable to you, to want to write you a letter a year from now,' etc. This exercise as metonymy for an interaction with wonder at its core—i.e., how can I be closer, nearer, more vulnerable. Friendship as nearness (re: distance, but also other forms of being near). (Am reminded that the endgame of ekphrastic writing is to take that mode of attention and wonder outside and apply it to the always world, in an each-day-is-a-museum kind of way. The impulse to thrill to friendship similar; poem befriending another poem as stand-in/placeholder for how we interact with anything we feel we can care more about, love, worry for, etc.) Befriending poem as poem, but also a way of being in the world, of loving the world. Final thrust of Hugo-inflected letter-poem writing—to remind how in the end I am always writing for you, specifically, whoever you are, wherever I am. There are things I want to say to you. Here are all my letters. Hope you are well. Wish you were here. Love, Tyler"

72.

I am looking at a picture of me with Tyler, Iowa City, summer, some months ago. Our arms are around each other and we are raising our arms to a street light.

73.

Were we both wearing pink shirts initially? No, he changed to match mine.

74.

So I wrote David and Jeff:

"Loves, Working on a prose piece that is maybe going into a quick section on friendship in poetry. I want to mention Bashō and Sora but don't have the right books right now. Would either/both of you be up for free-handing a quick salve from memory, a brief/casual explanation of B&S and why or how we'd ever always care about them? I'm thinking this could be research in the spirit of. If you are up for or could care! With more for, more cares, Z"

Three weeks later, I received the following report. The epistolary equivalent to a quarterback under no pressure except from the blitzing scent of clover throwing a five-hundred-yard intentional grounding. The ball is now in the parking lot.

The field is everywhere.

There Will Be Medicine in This Again

by Jeff Downey & David Bartone

In this mortal frame of mine which is made of a hundred bones and nine orifices there is something, and this something is called a wind-swept spirit, for lack of a better name. —Bashō

Everyone here knows the story. —Sora

The story of Bashō's *Oku no Hosomichi*, best translated as *Narrow Road to the Interior*, is painful to summarize in its simplicity. Bashō, believing himself unable to make a worthy homage to the masters without visiting the land they frequently wrote of, set North. For five years after returning, Bashō worked on his manuscript of the account. Sora, his student and companion, went also and wrote his own version of the journey.

When Zach told us that he was working on a prose piece about companionship in poetry and asked if we wouldn't mind talking about Bashō and Sora—"why or how we'd ever always care about them"—we thought it would be appropriate to compose this not as a dialogue but as a continuous thing (essay/haibun/eclogue), our questions and answers implied in the linking devices: paragraph breaks, excerpted passages, flights of fancy.

Companionship is not as much an intersection as the length of track that intersecting lines share (often at or near rail stations, in the metaphor; in reality, more likely on the long, conversant stretches of time). The form of companionship is rather uncomplicated, like hope. You have lost your way or a parent, or asked of friends who have the icons that appear to them along such a search for. Understanding. At such times a Sora is crucial and may appear. A Sora is want for little. A Sora gains your company. Not Bashō's ultimate empathizer but the lasting (for at least a little of the pilgrim's metaphoric while) accompaniment is Sora. He appears along Bashō's, but with his own, as it is an honor to have friends who compel. For you in turn to. The poet among friends does not have to have visions. Good conversation is a mind, welcomes digression, can't keep so much a secret (because it would be from itself) as a context sacred, as Dante in the company of Virgil:

So we moved toward the light, and as we passed
we spoke of things as well omitted here
as it was sweet to touch on there.

To dip into Bashō's prose is to find many wonderful stories about friends building homes for him, hosting gatherings to celebrate his work, taking care of him when he was ill, and of course accompanying him on his travels. It's one of the great paradoxes of his work, how his ethos is that of the man who straddles this world and the spiritual one, venturing out on isolated, soul-searching journeys, yet the final product is always a little bit raucous, a kaleidoscope created of the tilted mirrors of Bashō's personal quest and the rough gems (those party favors) of his companions along the way. Sometimes it is almost hilarious how generous Bashō can be, as in the case of *A Visit to the Kashimi Shrine*, the second of his major travel sketches, wherein Bashō himself only writes eight of the twenty featured poems, really more of an anthology than a work by a single author. But this is not the notion of an anthology in the Western sense, one that groups poets around some centralizing premise, but that of an event that must be written about together and then curated.

Bashō's travel forms are stark. They produce a sort of glare that prevents looking elsewhere for comprehension, a limit—a call to awaken one's sense of ever-sought, ever-present myopia—that exists in relation to Sora's existence.

The first mention of Sora in Bashō's work (found, albeit, in our limited access to English translations) occurs in the climax of *A Visit to the Kashimi Shrine*. Inspired by a favorite poem about the full moon, Bashō has embarked on his visit to the shrine in hopes of seeing the moonrise over the mountains, but rainy weather foils his plan. After staying awake all night to see the moon and catching only glimpses between clouds, Bashō and his companions try to console themselves by writing some linked verse. Mostly, these poems are tough-luck poems, contemplating the nature of a missed opportunity, but Sora's stands out as a deliberate revision of Bashō's preceding haiku. Here is the exchange:

Having slept
In a temple,
I watched the moon
With a solemn look.

(Written by Tōsei, Bashō's pen name at the time)

Having slept
In the rain,
The bamboo corrected itself
To view the moon.

(*Written by Sora*)

The genius here is Sora's wilding. It turns the temple into rain, the
moon-gazer into bamboo. But this is not just metaphor; it is action.
(To call the bumblebee a metaphor is to risk the next crop.) Sora's
echo lends variety and bearing. The plant's work of finding light is
solemn, but then so is solemnity a kind of basking joy. And what is
the work of the poet but to bask in paradox? The companion who
dares to respect ambiguity while chasing truth is Sora. Love him,
spirited here in Pound:

The blossoms of the apricot
blow from the east to the west,
And I have tried to keep them from falling.

Bashō watched the moon this way, while Sora watched the moon
and Bashō. This way the scene is given its countenance. It is a kind
of respect for the world that the poet, wondering why the moon rises
with such melancholy, observes. In making a fugue of his own and of
the others' ability to see and say and sing, Bashō's travelogues are the
anthology of ghosts and companions. It's why he gets upset when he
can't remember what an influence wrote about a certain haunt, and
why he comes off only half-committed to seeking enlightenment—

because he is not willing to clear his mind. He knows he belongs to a tradition, which makes him backward-looking, which in turn makes him prone to sentimentality.

But there are many ways to be a Sora. There was the time Zach was sitting on our weight bench benching, while one evening we composed our poem "Case Study for There Will Be Medicine in This Again"—part of the phrase he later appropriated. We don't re-member quite how much of the original festival of composing Zach was participant to, or whether he was privy to in periphery, and the intimacy of not remembering such distinctions very well is much of Sora. Our festival of the poem occurred, and Zach's occurred in exposure then and in full at some point later, on the same or similar altar with the same drink. Alter, so to speak. For how long could our festivities be expected to go on without the accompaniment of another in his utter, individuated aloneness?

"See you Soras later," for example.

"I'm some real Sora shit," a note left on the bedroom threshold before canned beer snoring up a friend's couch, the Honda packed outside, trunk full of breakup.

"To say more is sacrilege." —Bashō

Sora: the name is one that is achieved. Sora among friends is achieved. On the first day of the trip to the deep north, the pilgrims shaved their heads, as was customary for protection, and dressed in Buddhist robes. They rubbed their legs with moxa, a medicine of wormwood that restores strength. Bashō, famously named after his house which was famously named for the *basho* (plantain tree) his disciples planted at the hermitage they also built for him, writes in his travel diary how he and Sora, once named Kawai Sogoro, anticipated the pleasures and hardships of the journey. Commencing together with their haircuts, Sora, who had previously "carried water and wood" at Bashō, wrote:

Head shaven at Black Hair Mountain we change into summer clothes

Bashō notes that when Sora shaved his head he changed his name to "Sogo," the Enlightened, and so, given his given name, "the 'changing clothes' in his poem is pregnant with meaning."

This is the precedent, then, that leads Zach to scribble in blue ballpoint, "(Soras)," in the margin of books found unpacking in the sad summer we all leave our home in western Massachusetts with pink-flowering spirea (*vulgo*: magic carpet) beneath the picture window and long sloping lawn. Tired legs, dropping the plow with a sigh, we sow marginalia, so that in our new homes, in our after-lives, unpacking books, Sora blossoms like money left in a birthday card. Specifically, this note, "(Soras)," bracing these lines in Richard Hugo's "Letter to Kizer from Seattle":

I'm back at the primal source of poems: wind, sea
and rain, the market and the salmon. Speaking
of the market, they're having a vital election here.
Save the market? Tear it down? The forces of evil
maintain they're trying to save it too, obscuring,
of course, the issue. The forces of righteousness,
me and my friends, are praying for a storm

In the spring of 2010 we co-taught a writing workshop at UMass
Amherst called "In Rare Forms: Collaborative Writing for the Event-
ful." We conceived of a reading list that had its own ambitions but
ultimately only led to studies in living a poetic life among such a
Sora as Zach. The Book of Genesis belongs, too, to that epistolary
tradition of writing incarcerated: for what is heaven but a constraint.

If You Get Lost Remember Where You Are. The parting words of a
ride to the airport become a poem. Bradley International Airport in
Hartford. In the afternoon means a quick stop by the teletheater to
watch the men, invariably, watching harness races. Odds on the sulky
in red. Odds on idleness. The parting images of a ride to the airport
become words. Epply Airfield in Omaha, opposite the Missouri River
from Fontenelle Forest. Lewis and Clark camped here and wrote in
their journals about strange albino catfish and the now-extinct yellow
wolf. Lucien Fontenelle, the forest's namesake, was a trapper who ran
a trading post nearby. The only extant picture of Fontenelle is a sketch
of him being chased out of the forest and into grassland by a black
bear. Ecologically, it's an area known as oak savanna, where prairie and
forest begin to blend: blue stem and bur oak, goldenrod and cotton-

wood. The parting words a poem, proper nouns parting with their instance of occasion. To write this now, three cycles after we've parted, seems like roll call of the ailments since, in enduring order: Crohn's, Lynch, melanoma, neuropathy, mania, depression, bedbugs, one black tick from that Leonberger that belonged to that meadow, a roll of the Interior die, Hippocrates, salmon run, pioneering, surgery, tomatillo husk, Zinc oxide, Objectivist, Black-eyed Lazy Susan.

Indeed such Sora among history is achieved—thus far less diminutive in meaning than most historic companions are awarded. Later histories will remind us, for example, that the success of Lewis's expedition predicated on his first decision in St. Louis to promote Clark to his equal in rank—Captain—upon recruiting him, so that the men would not pursue any opportunity of cleaving by an assumed imbalance of power. In the annals now the coin is set for the two names together: Lewis and Clark. Such is the familiarity with which a reader of Bashō will gain in the phrase "Sora wrote."

75.

This originally happened a while ago, not in the real time of this composition, though I maintain the real time of this composition as fact and frame. Around the same time, I started telling people I was interested in the present moment, whenever I had to tell people I was interested in something. The beautiful thing about being interested in the present moment is how presently everything applies. Just this morning, for instance (it is always just this morning, whenever I read), this poem by Nico Alvarado made the case for me:

Literary Criticism

I'm tired of everyone talking
about how all there is
is gesture and yet
gestures are all I know
to make. I mean
I don't mean.
I mean I do,
but. I mean
meaningful without
meaning. The gesture alone
is beautiful. Every effect
a side effect. Someone
carrying a box
with complete integrity.
Falling with it, even.
Who cares about cargo.
This woman I know, she walks
in a drainage ditch
with complete honesty.
Head up, shoulders back.
Who cares where
she's going?
But I do.
She's coming to my house,
which is our house.

Walking up the street.
Up the steps.
Opening the door
with grace and beauty!
Stepping in! Stepping in!
Stepping into my arms!

76.

In the present, the house becomes our house. At times, reality comes
closer. Just in time. I haven't seen Nico in a decade, but I know him
enough to know he knows Ron Padgett's "Louisiana Perch" and
won't mind my noting that his poem is friends with it. The Padgett
poem moves from lofty profundity to thinky gag to a short-order
catalogue of the same thing again and then again, a parody and
perfection of eros and lyrical posturing:

like the waitress, a

beautiful slender young girl!
I love her! Want to
marry her! Have hamburgers!
Have hamburgers! Have hamburgers!

77.

See the end of Hugo's "Degrees of Gray in Philipsburg," I might say in a class. I might say, the structure of these poems recalls the structure of that scrappy blip of ballad that came first in the first anthology I owned, the ditty that goes:

Western wind, when wilt thou blow?
The small rain down can rain.
Christ! That my love were in my arms,
And I in my bed again.

78.

Three norths: head, heart, body. At play in each of these poems. (A poem isn't about what you think or how you feel, it's about how you feel about what you think and what you think about how you feel, said one of my teachers. I could've left the room and thought about that for two years, called it an advanced degree.) Next let's list other ways a poem can develop by having the compass shiver and lunge from head to body to heart to head...

79.

Next let's compare the end of "Louisiana Perch" ("Have hamburgers! / Have hamburgers! Have hamburgers!") to the end of Robert Hass's "Meditation at Lagunitas" ("*blackberry blackberry blackberry*"). Next, half the class eats hamburgers for a week, half eats blackberries. All this happens in the first three minutes of class.

80.

Diving makes the water deep. One says. Completely true and not.

81.

It doesn't stop, is my main idea, even in this state, all this energy, even in this hobbled, desolate station, I want you, so much, whatever you are. Just this afternoon, for example, I woke with a thought about metaphor. How it cares for one thing. By yoking it to another. Even if you don't care about either thing you see the attempt to yoke—the attempt *is* yoking—and the care in it and you can care about that.

82.

Thus, I realized that when making a simile one could say *exactly like* instead of *like*, foregrounding that things are really not like each other at all, highlighting the distance, impossibility, ardor of the attempt ("my face lit up *exactly like* a Christmas tree"—it didn't, but you are trying to tell me, to get a message through), so a reader understands how much it matters to you to suggest the similarity, beyond accuracy, how much this joining means.

83.

I describe it to Lisa:

"Related moment: was reading Roethke yesterday, trying to find the lineation for a quote, got this loveliness instead: 'Waking's / Kissing. / Yes.' What is the tone of that yes?? A kinda 'exactly like' moment: waking is NOT kissing, we know, or not always, not only, not exactly, so saying 'yes' after insists, shows the invitation/need which tries to make it so. Willing. Saying 'yes' or 'exactly' is redundant, as content, so becomes pure immoderate intent."

84.

Merrill, again: "Anything worth having's had both ways." Which one could take at least multiple ways. And again: "The poet quotes too much? Hmm. That is / One way to put it."

85.

"The indirect purpose or, perhaps, it would be better to say, inverted effect of soliloquies in hell and of most celestial poems and of all music played on the terraces of the audiences of the moon seems to be to produce an agreement with reality."

STEVENS

86.

A memorial reading after the death of Koch. After the death of Rich. After the deaths of Šalamun, Edson. Donald Justice. Hillary Gravendyk, Jake Adam York. Stephen Berg's, in summer, my predecessor at the University of the Arts, in my white shirt and the jacket I keep on the back of my office door, as how many professors before me. Others I missed, and miss. Here we are. You can read whatever you like at the memorial, in any voice you choose, any location, for years and years.

87.

For a while I was writing a book about teaching called *Made of Feelings and Toys*. Creative writing as a method of inquiry: a way to revive the liberal arts. To lead indirectly everywhere. This will have to do.

88.

Hurt into memory.

"And much work still to be done. And the smell of ripe peaches. And Long-Jin tea. And lungs full of words. And being an opaque body that intercepts the rays of the sun."

ROSMARIE WALDROP

89.

That I often misremember the myth of Marsyas. Flayed for challenging the god. At lute? I don't believe in any version he was a singer. But I picture him wandering after he healed, or healed enough, if you can ever heal enough, singing. Those are the songs I want.

90.

Sarah Manguso: "The kind of music I want to continue hearing after I'm dead is the kind that makes me think I will be capable of hearing it then."

91.

It applies to any day. The kind of music I want to hear tomorrow, Sunday, March 15, 2015, after three days of steady writing and rain on the window and night sweats and fever and pills, is the kind of music that makes me think I will be capable of hearing it then.

92.

Oppen: "Surely infiniteness is the most evident thing in the world." And: "Let it be small enough."

93.

Having lived by poetry. I didn't know I'd never kill myself until I read Robert Hass's "Old Dominion" ("I begin making resolutions: to take risks, not to stay / in the south, to somehow do honor to Randall Jarrell, / never to kill myself"). The words gave me my life.

94.

That even now, most nights I repeat a small prayer from one of the first books of poetry I owned, by Richard Jones: "All this, my heart promises, tomorrow."

95.

Even now, in exhaustion, pain, increasing dismantlement, the subject is not exactly exhaustion, you can summarize it, sure, but then? Once a day, the light is pink on the shed. I am roasting a chicken downstairs. Though my appetite is small, I will prepare a feast. I have fried the liver in the pan I readied the stuffing in. I will save the bones.

96.

Richard Jones: "I don't care how small the ember is you give me—it will start a fire" (line breaks in there somewhere, wherever you like, put them in the air with a slashing hand).

97.

I get so caught up reading poems I forget when I last took my pills, if I just took one, I decide to drink coffee to see if I can get excitedly caught up further, why not, while we can, while we can, writing with action movies playing and a stack of books, Hilary asleep, sleep well.

98.

With hiccups not yet as bad as the hiccups my father had, dying, which still rattle, pain, to recall. I can't but cry out. And how in his last weeks, his mind painfully remaining, he didn't sleep. I'd stay up talking with him until my wife would wake and she'd talk to him. It was exhausting and then it was done.

99.

I often speak to him at night, speaking to trees through the window. I turn to the kitchen counter and imagine how pleased he would be to see these oranges, this dish with salt in it, to recognize it as salt and not sugar, to taste it to make sure. Then to taste it again. First with the spoon, then with his thumb.

100.

I imagine him traveling, as he never could in life, hiding out in Istanbul, in Cairo. When I ask him for advice, he says it will all happen every way you can imagine and more and astound you.

CHAPTER IV.

WASTING DISEASES

"HORIZON IN...   ...THE PAIN...   ...OF A DOVE."

1.

That the boy rises very early and sits reversed on the sofa facing the bay window looking for the bus to round the corner in rain.

2.

That when the bus appears the boy shouts and the mother and the sister begin shouting more and the sister is hurried swearing through the door.

3.

That the mother turns to him, haggard, and says I'm sorry I'm sorry if you are going to be a writer use all of this.

4.

The mother facedown in the hall, her head at the speakers. Pet Shop Boys very loud.

5.

That the sister's disability isn't a word you can say, it is an experience, is life. The boy rages against depictions of the disabled on TV. Angels here to teach us simple lessons about simplicity. When his sister's experience is often suffering, choicelessness, fear. And more real in real ways than lessons or angels.

6.

That the sister's condition grows worse after the father dies. "Is that bread or my brain?" she asks. She thinks everyone is somebody else in a mask, a wig. It is unclear what to hope for.

7.

He cringes when students in graduate school, in Massachusetts, praise poems that use the language of madness for aesthetic effect, for humor. The teacher asks everyone to bring in a poem with a notable ending and three people bring in poems by a kinda surreally poet who's cool that year, they praise how crazy, how nonchalant, these cartoonish declaratives of a limited world. One brings in an older poem: to laugh at a locution that has aged into awkward contemporary slang. Lighten up. The boy writes a poem called "Loving Chaos Enough to be Orderly, Loving Order Enough to be Ecstatic."

8.

As a child, he fights anyone who says "retard." Avoids alcohol, drugs, caffeine. Seeing how close we are to one another, that is, to becoming another, beyond us. Ability being only memory, peripheral clarity, the ability to pass. One gene or instant away. Is another shore.

9.

The mother is a weaver, tapestry artist, maker of giant felt pool balls on a whim. After the father dies she removes a large painting from its frame (very '80s painting, three cats dressed for dinner, bought as a joke, era his parents had jokes, parties, Talking Heads and Blondie, his mother's simple costume one Halloween: the killer!) and positions a small plastic bicycle on its wire.

10.

That the sister was born when the parents were very young. Dropouts from college, living wherever, sold bread they made (is that only legend? how many times did it happen? his mom confirms: "Yes, we really made and sold bread—four weeks? before we realized how labor intensive and unprofitable it was"), moved to Vermont because someone needed a car delivered, to Rochester where his mother studied art before growing annoyed at the era's pieties. To northern Michigan, where the sister is born, where his father could complete a degree (he was closer to finishing). In forestry. Which somehow, in a way that seems impossible a generation later, led to working in economics in the Carter administration, to a life in international trade and community development.

11.

The boy is born eight years later. He doesn't understand why his parents would have another child. Of course he knows the answer (love, willingness, foolishness, life, what the grave says the nest denies), but he doesn't understand.

12.

As his friends begin to have children, he wonders how many would
be willing, really, to devote the rest of their lives to caring daily for
a child—constantly attending to, bodily, no redemption, just the
passage of time, suffering, love, hoping to live long enough for your
child to suffer less than she inevitably will after you die, for you to
both end in the same old-age facility and thus suffer together as long
as you can. And how could you have a child if that was not also what
you were willing to do, meaning, what you, in some ways, wish for.

13.

Of course he loves his wife and loves the thought of seeing her with
a child that is theirs, of course, he feels that, too. But he would not
care for a child with his sister's condition for the rest of his life, he
knows that, or would not wish to, and he could not in good con-
science add to the world's pain, or the risk of it, to that degree, or
to even a lesser degree. Others know these risks as specifically as he
does and choose differently. And many do not and choose differently.
Fine, fine, fine. He does not know if he is correct in this thought and
feels more implicated than proud.

14.

Will someone call these thoughts "anti-disabled," "ableist"? He
means more to say we are all already in this. How much we are all
inches from one another.

15.

That neighbors, some caretakers, doctors, treat his forty-year-old
sister like a child. As though she needs to be educated, to learn,
leave the stage she's in. And will grow and improve. People believe
in improvement, to smile and praise and inspire progress. Often
such efforts hurt her further. The goal is the closest to stability any
moment can come, as things are, not to solve this problem. His sister
is not a child or a problem. People laugh at her non sequiturs: her
language has always worked as a kind of game, given in units for
certain responses, and now its links to communication are loosening
looser. The neighbors come with toys and they laugh when she says
she has an "intoxication of the breast" and bends for a shadow on the
floor she says is her tooth. She is very exhausted after.

16.

He has often hoped she would die, or at least die before his mother
does, so his mother might have some years not devoted to caring.
Neither correct nor proud to think this, and yet.

17.

By now it is unclear what's the sister's condition and what's the effect
of drugs or of drugs prescribed for the effects of drugs or the effects
of effects of drugs she has taken for forty years and don't forget her
father who was also her caretaker daily for forty years is dead.

18.

If the mother had died first. Would the father have kept caring for
the sister? If he had kept working, he would have needed more help.
You wouldn't blame him for instead choosing to suffer it differently,
travel to Istanbul, to Cairo. Or to give all money for her care and disappear. You wouldn't blame anyone for anything. But, no, of course,
he would have stayed, suffered it, loved, wouldn't he have?

19.

Will someone say the boy should care for his sister, devote his life, as
his mother has? But he could as reasonably devote his life to others
who are suffering, devotion that might have more effect. If his goal
were to devote his life to the reduction of suffering. It would be reasonable to devote it elsewhere. If we do not see the world merely as
blood, as blood. If we believe many problems of the world come from
seeing the world merely as blood, as blood. (Family comes first, I did
it for my family—as though that justifies, think of the history of such
justifications, brutal.)

20.

His sister doesn't have the genetic mutation he has and his father
and grandfather and probably great-grandfather and two cousins in
Oregon have. A relief, because how could she bear the colonoscopies,
other scans, the even further medical requirements.

21.

He is five and playing with his sister in the house in Michigan with potato bugs under the stones and raspberry bushes and bees in the lavender, and he realizes he is suddenly the older brother, she is playing in a way he has passed. In photographs it is clear, her condition is obvious, but he of course didn't see it. Fought friends who mentioned it. Said, and meant, very early, when the parents of friends offered pity, that it was simply how it was, normal, his sister.

22.

His parents shielded him. Just today his mother offered to come visit, stay in a hotel by the hospital, afraid he thinks she loves his sister more.

23.

It isn't surprising that this is a child who spent most afternoons reading by the river. Felt language communicated mostly an experience of a moment, a state, does not exactly refer, does not fix things in place or state, doesn't solve or reduce. Who often felt we are all one inch from another shore.

24.

That when he was in high school she lived briefly in a group home. He and his parents went to Tucson, their first real vacation. Orange trees, a jazz club. She stayed several months, gained thirty pounds, needed gallbladder surgery, smelled in unwashed clothes, was forced to do activities she couldn't, came home and was worse. Similar attempt and results a few years later. These were the best places.

25.

Her handwriting is worse again, she has forgotten how to color in the lines, smears across the page, has started reading books for the youngest, spends days with plush toys on the bed, TV and radio on, fears, a few days a week goes to a center where she has lunch and helps sort thrift-store piles, it is one of the best places. The mother hopes for moments in which the sister's "old" personality comes through.

26.

Oh but Mother (he begins in the evening) there is also mercy in the world, I have seen it. For one evening in Switzerland having left a woman on a coast gone north despondent there were no hotels I could afford which was a luxury also to be there to have a budget (this is before phones with the internet of course so a traveler arrived late and found a bar and made friends and asked where to stay) so I planned to walk all night and sleep by the river—I assumed every city had a river—but instead at an overlook met Swiss teens calling one another fuckhead in three languages who loved me because I was American and football and rap music and gave me rum and got me high and in the morning I left their apartment and watched old men moving three-foot chess pieces in the square, moving them delicately into crates there just for that purpose when it started to rain and someone practicing saxophone in a doorway nodded.

27.

For (he begins in the evening) there is also mercy also for example in Cinnecittà the film studio in Rome where Fellini preferred to recreate Rome to film Rome the only place in Rome allowed to make replicas the exact dimensions of the originals if you see a pieta or river god anywhere else it's a little larger or smaller than you think.

28.

For also in Cinecittà they save everything saving everything the essential hope of film for example a submarine in increasing disrepair waiting until someone needs a submarine in this exact instant of disrepair.

29.

Or for instance in New Zealand garlic bean sprout noodles in an alley in Dublin suddenly realizing I'd been taking the long way to a place around the corner from the apartment and a quiet bar.

30.

It is brief but no less real. Even what barely happens once happens and even the most that happens barely happens once.

31.

For on a shore my beautiful friend saying the world loves me so
nothing bad can happen to me and I heard she loved me considering
my considering her worlds.

32.

For a side door from the locker room I exited from always in high
school for a precise vision of gulls on the soccer field it was everything I wanted at the threshold.

33.

For in teaching learning whenever I could dismiss a student's ideas
professorially to instead ask a question and listen I am surprised.

34.

For I sometimes bring up the 1998 film *After Life* you have died and
need to choose one memory it will be your eternity produced by a
haphazard film crew what would you choose is this the heart of art
to preserve or recreate or create anew could you choose a memory
that never was or was for less than an instant of false thaw I always
choose moments of threshold, brink, perhaps not to preserve but
to feel oneself already savoring and moving further. In the hotel
my friend and I put on our jeans again for the pleasure of rubbing
against each other in jeans with nothing under them.

35.

For could you recreate an entire world—not the entire world, but an—from the art that matters and live there we already do.

36.

Mother your sentences ever winding toward their subject Latinate or is it Germanic revealed later a syntax I have adored though I'm sorry on the phone sometimes I am restless I think it has been a long conversation I have hardly talked to you at all.

37.

I remember you and my father playing baseball with a frying pan and an orange.

38.

You gave me the Marx Brothers earliest and didn't teach me how to make salad dressing but that making salad dressing should be effortless.

39.

Tonight I am staying awake while I can. I don't think I could sleep from these drugs or this pain but I am telling myself I am staying awake while I can.

40.

What would you save from the fire I would save the fire.

41.

My wife downstairs watching a film mixing a drink I should join
her but first I want to write another sentence that she will read in a
different year.

42.

Darwish is pacing with me in this room, he has been here in the
translation of Berger and Hammami:

I saw René Char
sitting with Heidegger
two metres away from me
I saw them drinking wine
not looking for poetry
The dialogue was a ray of light
And there was a passer-by waiting

43.

And: "I sang in order to feel the wasted horizon in the pain of
a dove."

44.

Apollinaire paces with me, he has been here: "I know nothing any-more and can only love."

45.

I leave the details to the details. There is something important about the hinge on the shed, I haven't had time to figure, I have a sense of it, something, something, of use or of something greater than use.

46.

That I am no different from my sister is how I feel at heart.

47.

I leave it, I leave it, even if I live you cannot drink from these waters so often with only your hands and a mess of feathers and return, not in the same life, even if you live, the snow is different, snow in the cathedral how does it get in though we don't wonder how the birds do they must carry it.

48.

Yeats: "I have prepared my peace with learned Italian things." No, I haven't, but I've been glad at times to be Antony leaving with his beloved ("You will be Rome"), heartbreak of metaphor how a lover is completely and also completely cannot be a city especially when you are charged with governing but I would gladly return instead to the river where my wife and I married standing in the shallows a dog leapt in to join us like a novel tossed into a lake.

49.

Screensaver of my soul those leaves in the light heightening to the point of obscuring their green.

50.

Mother I know we are both talking to my father constantly does he tell you what I say? The belt I married in was his I still use it my wallet was too.

51.

Once in Detroit he showed me the neighborhood where you lived and met in your teens it was boarded liquor stores nail salons not that different from the neighborhood in Philadelphia next to our neighborhood but he showed me here is the park and here is where we caught the bus and to get to your mother's house (it was only the present, ever) you start walking.

52.

Proudest out of all I have written of the lines I texted him before
one of his surgeries from a poem I had written that morning:
"Given such a tremendous sail, who alive would mind who alive
would mind who alive would mind the smallness of our boat?"

53.

(stopped by anger for a spell—would've liked a longer reprieve
before recurrence—not an eternal one—but some)

54.

(and yet simultaneously feeling—everyone who meets me should
know about my illness, its history—and yet not identifying, seeing
myself, as a "cancer patient" or "survivor" or one on a "cancer
journey"—a line from one of Andy's old poems in mind: "The
condition was / Fuck the condition")

55.

I am sorry if you need to outlive me.

56.

Thinking of how in one ancient period one with permission could remove as much marble from existing ruins as one could in a day, a kind of controlled preservation/demolition/mutation. Days, thus, were units of loss. You could walk them off.

57.

Can you read my tone altering already and in every word further, having in this text enumerated gripes and pettiness and pedagogies and so I am now moving toward. Toward what? At this distance in these dimensions every step any direction is toward. The universe still writes with one shadow and very gentle ink.

58.

The lake swims out. That my mother stood watching fireworks through the curtains, bright in the near pines.

59.

Or Pliny, on a ship, unable to reach shore to rescue his friends in Pompeii. He died not from the ash but in sight of it.

60.

And how often should heart tonic be consumed? As often. In every form you might.

61.

That I have always acted as though the best writing is ahead,
the poems that matter, I tell every class, are the next, the love
we love when loving, even now, is, as David said, the childhood
of the love we ought. How lovely to meet you older, to see ages
through us.

62.

And suddenly there is only fifteen minutes left in the film, and
you know the last minutes will be the credits, and at the very end
a list of the songs. Pause the screen a while, read it to me.

63.

Mother I would love to stay up even longer—as long as we can—
and read Inger Christensen's *Alphabet* with you.

64.

You showed me how to draw a stone well and the bucket in it and
the water in a single and enduring stroke.

65.

I wake and write some colleagues:

"I'm afraid I need to share some news from the last week that will become more complicated…"

My auto-signature:

Zach Savich
Assistant Professor, Poetry Coordinator
BFA Program in Creative Writing
Division of Liberal Arts
The University of the Arts
Office: Terra 809

66.

Wishing to be more public this time, this cancer, to go out, if I do, corresponding with everyone, not miss a chance to tell even the newest friend love.

67.

Worse today, queasy, very afraid of vomiting, since simply breathing is horrible, even with drugs, and coughing and hiccupping and laughing excruciate. I've been about to sneeze several times and the body protectively circumvented. Ginger ale, crackers, pacing. Animal fear and loneliness, a loneliness from the fear, from the body being a room you can't escape. Fastened to a dying animal? Not just fastened to it: I am it, tagged.

68.

I cancel the vision appointment don't order a new phone don't grade some papers. Will this be the last week I can climb the stairs? Will there be a day I realize I will not see our rowhouse's third floor again, will I live on the second, between futon and bathroom, until I climb down a final time? Surely that is possible, accept it.

69.

And yet. If you asked me to imagine at sixteen, at twenty, my ideal life, to design it. I would not have known how to imagine this life so well. I want to tell my students that, impossibly, luckily, it all followed poetry, reading and writing intensely, just that and so much fortune, led to these friends, travels, a job I love, friendships' endless seminars. That I was right to ignore everyone who told me you need to be cynical to network from more than honest enthusiasm to condescend to foreshorten. I know effort/work isn't enough, as a rule, that hard work mattering relies on lots of other matters, and yet.

70.

On a train to New York, 2010. I had just learned that my second book of poetry would be published. *Annulments*—my favorite of my first three. Will you read it and think of me? Snow out the window of the train, reading the *Purgatorio*, beside Hilary as she edited her novel. Borrowed apartment near Washington Square. She was wearing particularly thick pink tights, a denim skirt.

71.

Read Dante first at M——'s house. So much I owe, also, to those who let me house-sit during my years between periods in graduate school. I'd stay on a friend's couch or rent a room for a month when the houses' owners were back, or travel, and otherwise—I read, wrote, took and quit jobs, could afford to, gratefully. Finished my first book there. Spreading the pages around the house. Until the poems were as good as they were going to be, and I had found the best sequence I was going to find, and I knew there were maybe three publishers who might be interested, or else I'd start over. When people ask me about "becoming a writer," I say things I believe but usually don't say are you willing to live oddly and cheaply and avoid signing a lease for ten years?

72.

Read a Shakespeare play each morning, then there was Dante, then all the art books in the house, lying on the floor listening to the records that were just simply there on a shelf, before walking to my job grading standardized tests. Took the long way to get more time in the fields flying with snow before my hours in the benign corporate lull, hunched in a cube, taking my lunch pacing a field covered in an ethereal interstate hum. When I was accepted to graduate school again so went.

73.

My wife's name on one of the first mass emails, seeing her at a welcome meeting. I positioned myself to be next to her, leaning against a radiator against a window. Very vividly her ears, hands winding a scarf, adoring gratefully when she was speaking so it was acceptable to stare and also to hear her.

74.

That I like the *Purgatorio* best, I used to say in banter, because it's closest to where we live. Effort can advance you, but not necessarily. Some of the reports about cosmology are true, others mostly show perspective. Abrupt song. Which passes the time as much as offering doctrine or praise. The tenderest.

75.

Started to reread it now but Torday came by with a smoothie. That I never finished *Walden*, in high school, because a friend came by to go swimming. I figured if I had learned anything from *Walden* I should stop reading, swim. Ward Lake, outside Olympia. Often a man there, his car radio on, drinking who knows what from a faded orange juice jug, lily pads.

76.

That in this illness I find myself drawn to the worst foods, chemical foods, as though a sick body needs the sickness of sick nutrition, sick culture, cheese curls, potatoes from a box, cheap salami, soda.

77.

That I teach at a place where I could teach lying on the floor and probably no one would mind, would listen, good discussion, roll with it, human. Thinking of Berryman taking a cab to class and having it wait outside and return him to the clinic. Still lecturing brilliantly, they say, though sometimes giving the same lecture twice in a row.

78.

That I Skyped with friend, positioned computers on our beds. Surprised not to smell her on my hands after.

79.

That I'm aware these days are harder on my wife, my mother, friends, than on me, in ways. I am drugged, choiceless, out of it. As after surgery I will be drugged, demolished. But she, they, will witness, be able to imagine, worry, suffer through, care, while also continuing their wider lives, all of which I will depend on and probably, thus, also resent.

80.

Feeling only now given all this that I might be able to finally begin writing something that matters. Even in this book—surely saying all I have said so far has just started to be the right preparation to say more and better.

81.

That when Dante recognizes a friend, a musician, in Purgatory, they embrace, and weep, then he asks his friend for a song, and moves on. But how do you move on after hearing that song.

82.

That Virgil washes ash from the pilgrim with dew he gathers with his palms. If the grass is dry wait with your hands in it through the night or longer until there is dew.

83.

(grateful for the friends who see me wince—and ask once if I'm all right—and when I wince again—continue speaking)

84.

You live your life in one direction they say but which life?

85.

Andy sends a book by Marosa di Giorgio. I am at the point when I stop taking another painkiller when I feel pain intensify, since the pain seems steadily intensified, and instead take them just here and there, plant the seeds here and there as you go, no time to rotate

crops for a future, so many prescriptions, clearly I am past self-per-
fection even self-preservation, the doctors prescribe everything, urge
me to not worry about getting addicted, just take what I need. She
writes: "That towering old woman who walked by our orange trees
one night with her long white gown, her hair in a bun. The butterflies that left us when they flew off to chase her." And, as Donald
Revell discusses in *The Art of Attention*, I find myself praying for
those butterflies.

86.

Everything you write happens all right.

87.

Loughran sends me his new manuscript. The first poem is called
"Kafka." It starts:

No one cares
about the painting of the orange rooster.
I hang it up, remember
whatever I want.

88.

Can't focus or sleep. Go on Facebook, scroll, scroll. Go off. Scroll

NYT. Go on Facebook. Scroll. A friend posts a post that serves for a moment as an answer (every answer is only a moment—therefore, every moment is an answer?):

"But today I want Rilke to speak—through me. In the vernacular, this is known as translation. (Germans put it so much better—*nach-dichten*—to pave over the road, over instantaneously vanishing traces.) But translation has another meaning. To translate not just into (i.e., into the Russian language), but across (a river). I translate Rilke into Russian, as he will someday translate me to the other world. By hand—across the river."

TSVETAEVA (AND JEAN VALENTINE / ILYA KAMINSKY)

89.

That my mother calls, offers to send a check, as though the first weeks of this new illness will exhaust our wages. I tell her give it to me in person another day. What can be offered. She offers to buy my wife a hotel near the hospital, to come up tonight.

90.

My wife returns with everything I wanted for any potential appetite and more so much sorbet and crackers pudding and fabricated nutritional shakes BBQ potato chips and ginger ale and juice the kitchen

crowds she said it made walking home hard what can be offered she
has and now has to work on an editorial project I let her go wanting
just to be near.

91.

That to learn humility you carry a slab until even the most patient
cry they can no more and by then have you learned and what and for
how long?

92.

But how could I die when I am so delighted in exhaustion and
pain to start a movie in which in the first shot Liam Neeson pours
whiskey into a coffee cup and stirs it with a toothbrush how can I die
when this is in the world?

93.

Up at four for my last chance to eat or drink for a while, a day of
scans. Two beautiful sandwiches on my wife's bread. (I was in the
habit of baking, then she did it one week, and the result surpassed,
something in how she handled the dough, just enough, something in
the shape or temperature of her hands.) Superb sage sausages from
the Reading Market. (Paradise is not artificial.) Ate too much, from
joy, afraid of vomiting, now. Widely afraid: that she will hurt her
ankle while on a run tomorrow and won't be back in time to drive

me to the hospital, that I'll never teach again, that we'll get a flat driving home.

94.

Meanwhile, poets online are upset! They are writing about topics I've read others writing and thinking about often better but because they are poets and I like poetry I feel obliged to care about what they are saying instead of the writing of those who are not poets. They are upset! They are saying we all need to have an opinion about this right now you are either with us or against us, and when a poet posts about a controversy from a week ago people say but what is your position on this week's newest controversy, as though we are all talking heads as though each poet needs foremost to be spokesperson about today's topic! No, they are saying the real problems in the world aren't the real problems in the world they are problems in the poetry scene and who is or isn't writing in which ways! They are writing poems you couldn't write parodies of because the parodies would look exactly like the poems and if you don't like these poems you are against everything we believe in! Also, MFA programs are ruining literature! It ruins literature for a person to have funding and health insurance and friends and earn an art degree for a couple of years! It somehow spares them from the "real world"! Corrupting the purity of ego! Like there was this professor who told me don't get an MFA, do real work instead, not understanding that an MFA was a great way I could avoid labor that would have otherwise become my life! He said I should be more like him—he'd gone to an elite college then traveled in Europe for a year on family money, sometimes pretending to be traveling on a budget or needing to walk all night and sleep by a river as an adventure, loving Rome more than his hometown, then had gone to an elite graduate school where an elite connection landed him a job teaching at another elite college! You never know how life will turn out, he said! He published a couple books through a personal connection and is often judging contests or in Spain!

95.

But poets online are upset! I am upset too! And one thing that's clear is how sentimental we are, if you define sentimental as how people sigh at a poem with a rose in it, without really reading the poem, and so people sigh or react to poems with the ideas they like or like having in them, or because people they like wrote them, without really reading the poem and the poems don't even need to be read! But I believe in being upset! But if they have ever read the good stuff, which is so much stuff and so many kinds of stuff with no paucity and no lack of complexity at all, why wouldn't we prefer the good stuff! Right now! Who am I even talking about! I don't know, I'm shouting! I'm only now learning how many really believe it is all a rigged game of personal connections and fashion thus better to be doing the fashionable rigging, for who knows what minor end, how unequal it all is to dying, how unequal dying is to the bigness of the world, how sentimental to be dying, what avoidance, what indulgence, what a poor excuse for an excuse!

96.

In the opening shots the hero either drinks alcohol, showing he is a broken man, or drinks water very obviously, showing he is a recovering alcoholic who will need to descend back into his dark, broken ways during the film. Maybe he will be stabbed in the liver and continue fighting, like it's nothing. Like what isn't.

97.

When they stabbed the long needle into my liver I cried out and writhed, could not control it. Did not think of Prometheus but kept repeating the day's mantra, glad I had planned for it, from Revell: "On fire escapes without a fire in view." In my mind more ecstatically with each needle, extraction of tumor to test, pain. Or at times counting to one, one, one, one. The stabbed hero would actually instantly fall. Can we see him as more heroic, somehow, for it.

98.

When I first had cancer it was caught quick. I wasn't surprised, after everything with my dad, waited until he died to get tested for the genetic mutation, then immediate scope, tumor (ugly alien hamburger on the clear film), colon removed a week later. All suffering of recovery. But now. Have to remind myself I haven't even had any treatment yet, though plenty of medical attention. So the worsening days aren't in response to anything except the worsening body. (Legs shaky tonight, sore all over, nausea—still very afraid of vomiting, vomiting ceaselessly, though I suppose that will happen, too—a fact—accept it—then let it go.)

99.

That the time between these entries grows.

100.

But no matter what I know this chapter will end with number one hundred, and then there will be a final chapter, I have already decided. I'm remembering when my wife and I left the cabin where we stayed for a week with David a few months before we were married. At least one day a week since then I haven't been able to sleep for the luck of it, all of it, grieving, pained, never solving anything, but still suddenly inordinately happy, alive. But before that, on our way home, we stopped at an Indian restaurant. It reminded me of a restaurant I went to once (alone, with a book of poems, season I lived in a dusty furnished room with dudes drinking on the front steps you had to push past, Seattle, decade earlier). Where in my memory I swear it I found a large metal staple in my curry. Pulled it out, set it on the paper napkin (folded it in the napkin), continued eating, paid, tipped, left. I didn't feel proud or thrilled at the adventure of finding a staple in my curry or witnessing myself being a person who found one, did that, got a story to tell. Rather, I found it, ate, paid, tipped, left. I swear I remember and preferred and would still prefer that exact evening air.

"THE KIND THAT...

...CHAMPIONS OF PLEASURE DRINK."

CHAPTER V.
The Living Year

1.

B—— writes:

"If, at some point, you'd like to steam, please let me know. If we go to the banya early'ish on a weekday we'd likely have the steam room to ourselves, and I could make you whatever steam you need: light, heavy, dry, moist, warming, deep heating, gentle, not-so-gentle, etc. It's fairly close to your house. I'll pick you up."

2.

Melissa writes:

"The tarot says the outcome is strength. And large plans."

3.

Cassie writes:

"I had dreams of you and Hilary last night, lots of them. I remember little now. In one we were hanging out in the apartment where I grew up. But it was the present, and you were sick.

"I blame all this on Rome. Some god there feels threatened by you, doesn't want you there. Isn't this the third time something bodily has prevented you from going to that city?"

4.

I had forgotten: before cancer kept me from Rome in 2013, and now in 2015, a broken leg stopped me in 2005. I think this, like everything that happens to me, also happened to Freud?

5.

Lisa writes:

"Woke throughout the night from a string of dreams wherein every time I opened a magazine it was to an ad for one of your books."

6.

St. Patrick's Day. I refrain from upbraiding the insensitive whimsy of the oncology tech in leprechaun garb, shamrocks on thighs, hurrying through the tests to get to a bar. This is your guide to mortal realms.

7.

The oncologist says, "Tumors have a heterogeneous composition." Offers an analogy for me to understand. You know the move: somebody assumes somebody's expertise in a field means they can understand things only through comparisons to that field? "You work at an art school. Imagine that a painting has some blue dots, some green, some yellow, some white, some brown, some red. They aren't all the same. Your tumor is like that."

8.

There's a painting of dots in my liver! (Over the next year, one of the worst parts—most stressful, most frustrating—will be this doctor's approach to information. Being literary, I assume you don't need to actually say, "Give it to me straight, doc," because that's a cliché, and shouldn't they simply do it? But she doesn't.)

9.

Full-time sick. Just days ago I resented the doctor who implied I was nothing but a patient, and now I am grateful for his being ready to be with me in this. Could it have mattered in the last months I'd published a book, toured, taught, lived. But now. What's now.

10.

NPR racism, in bubbly tone: "There's a lively debate about whether ISIS and the attacks of September 11th represent Islam." A lively debate among idiots.

11.

Honor (and pain) of having the direct numbers of doctors, to have them phone daily, call any time.

12.

Napping drugged. Vision of doctors in coats at each side. It's hard not to respond. One says hold on, I'm calling in some others.

13.

Loughran writes:

"What I can think of is, send me a list of things you don't want me to start bringing to you guys, and I will start bringing everything not on the list. Among other things you are about to be on the curry list unless you put curry on the other list.

"Cavafy has this line I just read about 'champions of pleasure.' Be one?"

14.

Other vision. Old man (tanned, thin) fixing a cocktail. Pours a full bottle of vodka into another full bottle of vodka, liquor consuming his arms. Will he light it?

15.

I don't mind when people say the wrong thing about illness, but people who think they know the right thing, the exact right thing to say.

16.

I'll sign "yours" to whoever writes.

17.

Vision. Garden plot in a courtyard at a tower's base. Courtyard is ruined, overgrown, too deep to clear it. Can still distinguish it from the garden, raked earth, trellis. Look up. The sky (long cloud) seen from the garden is superior to the view from the tower.

18.

I reply to a student: "I think it means running between two seats of a teeter-totter, one marked WILD EXPANSIVENESS! the other FOCUS."

19.

My wife pours a whiskey: "Drinking for two now."

20.

That I still find pleasure raging at bad writing. Keats: "Yet I ride the little horse." A friend suggests subscribing to a political magazine, *Jacobin*. In our first issue's hundred pages, "neoliberal" and its variants appear fifty-one times. Multiple times in single sentences: "Mitchell argued that neoliberal programs are implemented to create test-case conditions for neoliberal policies." Another article tells us that—get this—*cell phones* are now being used for more than talking, which supports neoliberalism. Also, SimCity is neoliberal. And the Olympics. The house style is self-serious, witless. Then I see someone is writing yet another "running and" book. Then a lit mag comes with one of those paint-by-numbers lyric essays people are apparently still writing: a shallowly researched topic (shallowness presented as lyricism, suggestive, to cut a fact off swollenly—), in pithily titled sections alternating with a shallow personal narrative, only obvious ideas we already know, probably about someone's illness or dead father or being a writer—

21.

Or pleasure in the inadvertently brilliant lineation of a church sign:

IF YOU CAN'T FEED ONE
HUNDRED PEOPLE FEED
JUST ONE MOTHER THERESA

22.

Jordan writes (I'd mentioned hobbies, do I need one, for this time, inability):

"I don't know what a hobby is? I'm terrible at them. The only hobby I think I've ever taken up is fishing off the Montrose Pier on Lake Michigan with Ryan, catching mostly these sick overgrown tadpole fish called gobies—an invasive fish originating from the Black Sea that eat all the coho salmon roe—but sometimes catching some gorgeous lake perch. And my other hobby for one year was at Iowa when I quit drinking, bought a couple of guns, and went shooting alone at some outdoor range north of the city. If any of those two hobbies strike you as something you just might wanna take up, lemme know and I'll share my teacup of knowledge."

23.

I like when two friends are planning an escape. But one gets impatient, starts to run a harder route, too soon. His friend stays alongside, shadow to shadow. Persuading him to stay, wait for the new moon, but willing to run with him if he continues, shadow to shadow.

24.

We've been watching for hours, and only now the opening music, serenely late, exactly on time.

…

There is not another life, it is inside this one.

Deciding. For submission, surrender. Rather than attempting conflict (as though—oppositional world, metaphors of battle, that would mean seeing the self, even the sick self, as an enemy). To give in, agree with, further than acceptance. Unto merging. And become something else.

Fecundity of the interior. Organs grow organs.

...

But you can't.

The un-sick can read, develop. The sick have—shadows on snow. If I left the best books in my office, so I may return. I read now from the sidewalk box. What have you left?

Last meal will be shadows on snow, shadows on grass. To request for my last meal an evening in a city I don't know. You order what they have and read this book you have found.

...

A while since I have. And how long until. Between those two thoughts: who's written me today?

Wishing you in a warm breeze, years. I'm with you, years, the warm breeze, forever is a small place.

Biscuits, gravy

Oranges
Beaujolais

…

Cottage of wildflowers. Odor of honey in the motion of bees. Is it enough to pause, in a memory of times that haven't yet.

For weeks in the cottage sensing an ocean is close enough, a quilt, hay in the fire, now starting. Applewood.

Children with songs of times that haven't now.

…

If the shirt has roses, the threadbare shirt.

Every honest book is a crisis. I don't say about a crisis. I say a crisis.

I wrote this book at a brink.

Seven months later, I asked David and Tyler to help my wife help me die if I couldn't help myself.

I have lived.

For seven months, I left the house only to go to the hospital.

Every day, I let something else go. It was astonishing, how much I could let go.

I listened to my wife and the friends who visited build a garden around me.

I had a taxonomy: there were palliative necessities, and there were copings, and there were diversions, and there were some consolations, and there were many appreciations and memories (losses), but there were few pleasures or active hopes, and then fewer. There was little ability or self or will.

We still called most nights a party.

I hope now to have a couple of all right years.

Friends came. Some praised me. More than ever, I knew that any-
thing they might praise, they had created. They had escalated and
forgiven and permitted and corrected and more and, please, more.
Jess Jeff Larissa Sam Caryl Caren Cassie Dan Dan Dan Callie Becca
Isaac David Tyler Michael Jay Sara Roy Sarah Annie Molly Patrick
Abby Natalie Josh Jensen C.S. Claudia Jacob Sydney Terry Trevor
Kathy and others appeared. I hope to have a couple of all right years
and to appear for others as they appeared.

I woke from a surgery I shouldn't have been able to have. Mark
was there. He brought me a rosary. I kept it where I could see. Not
because of religion, but because of Mark, Mark Leidner.

One writes not to express but to move beyond. You can't.

I think of the birds that sing not to be heard but to continue.

Or those that nest in shopping carts. It isn't art, exactly.

Much of me is still in the chemo chair, still cut open, still in a year
of drugs and TV and each day worse, and in two years before that of
what I had thought was the worst. Enough bad days, bad enough,
that no number of good ones can balance them. I feel simply. We do
not grow more intact. What do we grow?

Hilary Plum is my wife and how simple it is, how much I couldn't have imagined her and have loved each day together and have survived for more. She was there every hour. I can't imagine.

I anger at literature, at art: how little of it feels worth having survived for. But some of it feels more worth having survived for than most things.

But before I survived, I wrote this, as a crisis, a brink. There is a book you write when you think you might not be able to write anything else. I reread it over the next year to convince myself that I had existed, and so I might still.

I am waiting to wake up one morning and feel a feeling I remember from before all of this. I know the problems with that wish.

ZS, Philadelphia, March 2016

Acknowledgments

Portions of this book appeared, in earlier forms, in *Crashtest, Euphony*, the *Fanzine, jubilat,* the *Kenyon Review Blog,* and *Seneca Review.* It shares a few phrases with my earlier book of prose, *Events Film Cannot Withstand* (Rescue Press, 2011), and with the poetry collection *The Orchard Green and Every Color* (Omnidawn, 2016). Nico Alvarado's "Literary Criticism" first appeared in *Handsome.* This book draws from many years of conversation and correspondence; I apologize for any borrowings that should be represented or attributed differently. Thanks to Patch for the art and to Lisa Wells for her early encouragement of the effort and to everyone at Rescue, particularly Sevy, for the graceful design. Thank you, also, to my students and colleagues at the University of the Arts, especially to Elise Juska, Connie Michael, Steve Antinoff, and Jay Baker. Finally, I'm grateful, ongoingly and daily, to Caryl Pagel.

Zach Savich was born in Michigan in 1982 and grew up in Olympia, Washington. He received degrees from the Universities of Washington, Iowa, and Massachusetts. His work has received the Iowa Poetry Prize, the Colorado Prize for Poetry, the Cleveland State University Poetry Center's Open Award, and other honors. His fifth collection of poetry, *The Orchard Green and Every Color*, was published by Omnidawn in 2016. He teaches in the BFA Program for Creative Writing at the University of the Arts, in Philadelphia, and co-edits Rescue Press's Open Prose Series.

CHRISTIAN PATCHELL

Christian "Patch" Patchell is a cartoonist, illustrator, designer, and all around creative collaborator. Patch has lived in Philadelphia his entire life and truly loves the city. He divides his time between making art, teaching, and collaborating with the Philadelphia Cartoonist Society. His art has appeared on everything from comic books to greeting cards. Patch is the author of the book *I Put the Can in Cancer: A Journey Through Pictures* and the creator of the award-winning animated short *The Brothers Brimm*. He is also the writer and illustrator of *Monster Mondays*, an online comic strip about creatively surviving.

RESCUE PRESS